Soundtrack
of SILENCE

Love, Loss, and a Playlist for Life

MATT HAY

WITH STEVE EUBANKS

ST. MARTIN'S PRESS
NEW YORK

First published in the United States by St. Martin's Press, an imprint of St. Martin's Publishing Group

www.stmartins.com

Designed by Gabriel Guma

Library of Congress Cataloging-in-Publication Data is available upon request.

ISBN 978-1-250-28022-0 (hardcover)
ISBN 978-1-250-28023-7 (ebook)

Our books may be purchased in bulk for promotional, educational, or business use. Please contact your local bookseller or the Macmillan Corporate and Premium Sales Department at 1-800-221-7945, extension 5442, or by email at MacmillanSpecialMarkets@macmillan.com.

First Edition: 2024

10 9 8 7 6 5 4 3 2 1

For Nora, Luke, Maddie & Kate.

That was going to be my whole dedication, but you deserve a bit more explanation here. Throughout the writing of this story, I was never uncomfortable sharing my personal experiences, except that sometimes my experiences were also your experiences, and none of you signed up for this. A few times I thought, I hope they aren't bothered by me writing my story. Driving home one afternoon, "Your Song" popped up on the playlist. Not surprisingly, Sir Elton John took what I was thinking and said it even better.

I HOPE YOU DON'T MIND

THAT I PUT DOWN IN WORDS

HOW WONDERFUL LIFE IS WHILE YOU'RE IN THE WORLD.

—Elton John

Soundtrack
of SILENCE

INTRODUCTION

SWEET DREAMS ARE MADE OF THIS

—Eurythmics

I F YOUR LIFE WAS MADE INTO A MOVIE, OR BETTER YET, A MULTIPLE-EPISODE LIMITED SERIES THAT PEOPLE COULD STREAM WHENEVER THEY LIKED, WHAT WOULD BE THE SOUNDTRACK? What music would set the pace and mood of your story? As the opening credits fell away and the first scene faded in—*overhead shot of a car on a narrow, straight country road*—what song would provide the overlay? Would you pick something like "Indiana" by the Samples—"*I remember the first time I drove through Indiana / Thinking to myself how big this land really is / Amber waves of grain, from a highway / Who lives in that house so far away?*" Just guessing, but I would say, probably not. Still, the question remains: What lyrics would flood you with memories of your own, or ignite an emotion buried under the dormant embers of time?

I remember cruising in the passenger seat of Stephanie Lake's Subaru on a summer evening in high school, many of my best friends packed around me singing Prince's "7" to the road signs and cornstalks standing tall as we passed by. *"No one in the universe will ever compare . . ."*

I remember reclining at my fraternity house on a perfect, lazy Sunday afternoon in April watching the Masters golf tournament on mute with the windows open, Trey Anastasio of Phish extending an invite to *"come waste your time with me."*

I remember an overcast, bone-chilling February, the kind of Midwestern day that makes you think you live at the North Pole, when my college roommate and I decided that instead of going to class, we had to take a road trip south to New Orleans. Neither of us had been to Mardi Gras. That was as good a time as any. We borrowed a car and mapped out a path, eleven hours and thirty-seven minutes, give or take time for gas stops and a meal or two. Not long after jumping on Highway 37, we realized we'd left the stocked CD case on the roof of the car, so we drove all those hours listening to Janis Joplin, the CD already in the car, confess that she'd *"trade all her tomorrows for a single yesterday."*

Flash-forward to a night in Chicago with my roommates, having just one more drink while marveling at the tight California harmonies of Brian Wilson's band. *"I'm pickin' up good vibrations."* Then zip ahead again to that moment on the way to the hospital for one of my surgeries, Bob Marley assuring me that *"every little thing gonna be all right."*

Those nuggets of life represent a past that has built the present and will hopefully shape a small corner of the future.

For most people, the first lick or two of a song will trigger a memory like the ones I've just described, a warm shower of feelings linked to a lyric or a beat. Songs are like pages in a scrapbook, each igniting an emotion from the past. But when that person whose life is laid out in those pages can no longer hear—when the sounds that jar the memories slip away like a friend's voice in a passing car—the scraps within the pages of that book suddenly stop. One page is filled with vivid recollections. The next is vacant and white, all the *"misty watercolor memories / of the way we were"* faded like photos in a ceaseless rain.

Deafness is hard to describe because it's impossible to simulate. Ears don't have eyelids. You can't remove your auditory receptors for an hour or two just to experience what it's like. Deafness is unique among the senses in that respect. If you want to know what it's like to be without sight, you can put on a blindfold in the dark and bump into things for a while. You can also get a shot of Novocain and marvel at the weirdness that comes with losing your sense of touch. If you have contracted a virus, there is a chance you lost your sense of taste or smell. Being deaf is different. You can simulate hearing loss easily enough. Put in earplugs and don a noise-canceling headset and you will muffle most sounds, but if lightning strikes a tree nearby, you are going to hear something. Even in your quietest moments, there are sounds: SUVs lumbering down your street, neighbors mowing their lawns, dogs barking, or the hint of a breeze rustling the Bradford pears around you.

Go indoors to the quietest place in your home, and you will still hear things: the patter of your own footsteps, the rasp of your own breath, or a late-morning growl from your stomach alerting you that it's lunchtime. Even if you pause those bodily functions, you might still hear the hum of electricity pulsing through wires. The point is, no matter how quiet you make things, hearing people hear, which is great. However, that makes it harder to appreciate those who can't.

Deafness remains foreign to most for good reason. Almost a million people in the United States can't hear anything. Those are the people who, without an assist from technology, couldn't hear a cowbell if you rang it behind them. That may seem like a big number, but in a country of 330 million, it's far enough down the list that it's reasonable to have never met anyone who is deaf. It's also worth noting that more than half of those who are completely deaf are over the age of sixty-five. That is quite different from "hearing loss," which affects well over 466 million people worldwide, with the number continuing to rise. Hearing loss falls on a wide spectrum, and you know plenty of those people. It's the guy in the office next door who has hearing aids that you never noticed until he pointed them out to you. It's your mom who is tilting her head and saying, "What'd you say?" more often than she did a year ago. It could be the girl on your daughter's soccer team with a quarter-sized disc attached to the back of her head and a wire that runs somewhere. You'd love to know more about her, but it's awkward to stare and scary to ask, so, like most people, you do nothing. All of them and many more live under the roof we label as "hearing loss."

Like millions of people in the world today, I live on the edge of that roofline, a world where the promise of technology keeps hope alive while the frustrations of loss tap me in the shoulder like a steady rain.

Everyone who lives inside the hearing-loss community feels walled off and lost at times. There are the sounds, for example, that the totally deaf rarely hear no matter how advanced the technology. Even with the miracle of modern cochlear implants and other artificial hearing-enhancement devices, a deaf person has trouble with words that lack hard consonants. If it starts or ends with the tick of a *T* or has the kick of a *K*, it's easier to fill in the blanks. Throw out a soft, swirling sentence and, even with the best technology on the market, the sounds come out like a lullaby in a foreign language: lovely, earnest, and meaningless to the person on the receiving end. In one of the many ironies of hearing loss, a question like "How's your hearing?" has no hard handles on which to grab. For many, it comes across as something like *"awe ooh zee."*

Since no hearing person can relate to total deafness, living in a world where you can't hear the soft snores of the person you love or the hard cheers of thousands for your favorite football team, try to ponder something simpler. I ask again: What would be your soundtrack?

I first pondered that question in my twenties, because I had to cope with the realization that I might never again experience the feelings of piling into a buddy's Jeep while Glenn Frey went to his upper register telling me about *"a peaceful easy feeling."* I created my soundtrack once Glenn and his bandmates began to fade like the light of a setting moon.

My objective in telling this story is to help others find their own connections within the quiet places of life; to hopefully make you ponder the moments, the relationships, and the feelings you never want to forget. If the rest of your life had to be lived in silence, what sounds would you want to remember?

For me, it was everyday sounds like the high-pitched growl of a chain saw as it bit through the trunk of a poplar. I wanted to remember my mother's voice calling us to dinner, and the folksy wisdom of my father, a woodshop teacher who gifted his homespun nuggets to my big brother and me growing up.

I wanted the laughs of the ones I love to always be embedded in the folds of my mind.

And I wanted to remember music, the catchy hooks that stick around in the brain for decades, like the baritone beat of Waylon Jennings as I played in the driveway, riding my Big Wheel and spinning out. *"Just some good ol' boys / Never meanin' no harm."* Dad would always holler at me (in southern Indiana, kids heard a lot more hollering than yelling, the former being a raised voice, the latter an angry one), because the Big Wheel left black streaks on the sidewalk.

I also needed to recall those moments in my youth when bad news marked a turning point, the feeling in the pit of my stomach when an otherwise quiet car ride was broken up by Bob Dylan knowing just the right words. *"Tangled up in blue,"* indeed.

Of course, there were first dates, first kisses, the first flutters of love seared into my brain with the Verve telling me, *"It's a bittersweet symphony, this life."*

Then there were the tender minutes a man has no words

to describe. Can you imagine losing all memory of your own voice whispering a beautiful baby to sleep? *"Blackbird singing in the dead of night / Take these broken wings and learn to fly . . ."*

Those moments are more than a playlist: they represent the pieces of a life no one wants to lose. For those reasons, I set out to create a soundtrack of my life, a "Matt's Greatest Hits"—not songs by me, but songs that connect me to moments I never want to forget.

Hearing loss is seen by most people as a physical disability, or "challenge," as it's known in the newest lexicon. There's nothing wrong with being deaf. Deaf culture thrives throughout the world. People everywhere find fraternity in their shared, silent experiences. That just wasn't my culture. Not only had I never met anyone who was deaf, the closest I even came to knowing anyone with hearing loss was my grandpa Earl, whose huge tan hearing aids remained unused and unmoved for a decade in the drawer next to the green rotary phone on his desk.

Even when my hearing wasn't great, I felt comfortable in almost every room I entered. New people and things, new interactions; it was all like a movie where someone sees Las Vegas for the first time, wide-eyed and smiling. Fear of losing that connection proved to be a powerful motivator. My soundtrack was a way to *"hold on loosely, but don't let go."*

This is also a love story, one with an unexpected focus on the "in sickness and in health" part and a dash of "for better and for worse."

There is a good chance that it is your story and your journey, too, whether or not you have all five of your senses. You don't have to lose your hearing to feel like you've been dealt a bad hand. Staying a step ahead of the terrifying darkness taught me that you don't always have to play the hand you're dealt in life. Sure, sometimes you've got to *"know when to hold 'em / and know when to fold 'em."*

But sometimes, in life, it's okay to ask for new cards.

ONE

HERE IS WHAT IT FEELS LIKE. Before becoming deaf, I could walk into any room and feel comfortable in my own skin. I have always been a natural conversationalist with a healthy curiosity. Where are you from? What do you do for a living? What sort of hobbies do you enjoy? Those were my questions, the topics I loved to explore with others. In turn, if you had asked me how I was doing, you'd likely get two stories and a movie quote, even though the question was perfunctory and you were hoping for a "Yeah, I'm doing well, thanks."

Contrast that with my social engagement now. Maybe it's a wedding reception. The second I walk into the crowded room, I turn into Jason Bourne, assessing my surroundings, locating the quietest spot in the room, looking for the escape routes, and calculating how many steps it will take for me to get out of any awkward situation that might arise. Then I survey the crowd. How many people do I know? How many know me? More to the point: How many know that I'm deaf? Of the people I do not know, who has facial hair and who doesn't? That's a big deal when it comes to lipreading, especially in bad lighting.

I check to see if there is a band or a DJ and run some calculations on when the music will start to play, as well as an educated guess on the volume level we can expect. If I need to say something like "Best wishes" to the bride or a quick "Thank you" to the parents, I'd better get it done before the music. Then I have to find our table and make sure I'm among the first to get a seat. Not only do I have to make sure a friend or family member is sitting next to me for cues, it's always best if the person seated on the other side is someone I know. Getting information from allies on both sides of a table adds another layer of insulation. Otherwise, the lights may go out.

I *see* sound as light and darkness, a visual representation of a sense that only exists in my memory. Imagine eight people at a dinner table, four couples at a close friend's birthday on a Saturday night. Seven hear fine, maybe missing something here or there, but nothing more than the normal misheard or lost word. But one person at the table is completely deaf with a big behind-the-ear implant processing sound electronically. Now, picture a spotlight above each of those people with the brightness corresponding to what they can hear. Right out of the gate, most of these lights are bright and remain lit, but the light over the deaf guy dims more and more as he misses things. Ambient conversations, the clinking of silverware at another table, or the low-grade roar that always accompanies the arrival of more guests—these short-circuit the deaf guy's ability to discriminate and categorize sounds. People who can hear well instinctively focus their attention on the conversation in front of them. They do this through visual and auditory cues that have evolved over thousands of years. But to the deaf guy, every additional sound is like a wave crashing on a drowning person.

Our deaf dinner guest makes the effort to steer the conversation toward a friend right across from him, something safe, like basketball. He says, "It's so great that the old coach came back."

"Yeah, it's a bummer, though, that—" The friend is interrupted and starts laughing at something the deaf person didn't hear. The light dims.

"Right, exactly," the friend adds to another person at the table.

The conversation ends. The deaf guest's light is out. He sits in the dark, left wondering: What was a bummer, and why? A normal interaction, one that only took a few seconds, ended with the deaf person frustrated and lost, part of an intimate group, but alone.

Our same deaf person might be engaged in a conversation, but if he drops a fork, he's faced with a terrible choice. He can bend over to pick up the utensil, but in doing so his light will go out. It's like being in a theater watching a gripping movie and having to go the restroom at a pivotal point in the plot. If you leave, no matter how fast the trip, you will either need someone to fill you in on what you missed, or you will have to fill in the gaps with your own best guesses. The deaf person with a fork on the floor can either lose the conversation, stop eating entirely, or decide to explain that he needs you to stop talking while he grabs the fork. On a case-by-case basis, this doesn't seem like a big problem, but on a typical night out with friends, a deaf person could face those decisions a few dozen times before the water arrives.

Keeping the light on can be exhausting.

No matter how wonderful and understanding your friends might be, after a while it's easier for you to check out, to flip the switch off. It's simpler to live your life in the dark.

To put some reality behind that, take the story of something standard and mundane. I went out to buy lightbulbs. Since I wasn't sure what style or size I wanted, I hit the Home Depot. We were still in the grip of coronavirus protocols at that time, so all the employees and a good half of the customers wore masks. A greeter said something at the front door, which I assumed was "Welcome" or "May I help you find anything?" but between the muffled sound from the mask, the clanging carts, beeping forklifts, and all the other chatter in a big-box store, I had no idea if words came out of this person's mouth or not. I just smiled and kept walking.

Once inside, I ran into a friend of a friend, someone I'd met once. She was keeping an eye on her kids while making conversation, which made it almost impossible to follow what she was saying. I nodded and smiled, tying to control the chat as much as possible because if I'm talking, I'm not having to listen. The more I say, the less likely I am to miss what is being said. The whole time, though, I was asking myself: How long is this interaction going to last? Do I have time to tell her that I'm deaf, or would that only extend this engagement beyond its normal lifespan? When she did speak, I nodded and smiled. I caught the word "rainbow" but walked away not knowing if she was talking about the new paint colors her daughter had selected or the bridge her aging dachshund had just crossed.

I've learned over time to be careful about facial expressions. Once when I was having a tooth filled, I nodded and smiled at my dentist and the hygienist when I had no idea what was being said. If you think following conversations behind masks is a challenge, imagine what it was like with all the high-pitched drills and yacht-rock music. A minute after my smiling encounter, the dentist started drilling without Novocain. I jumped from under my paper bib and yelled. It took another beat for them to realize that each had asked me separately if the other had given me the shot, a hard lesson that nodding and smiling is not always a neutral or even safe response.

In the Home Depot conversation, I did my best to keep my expressions neutral while also appearing to remain engaged. Thankfully, it didn't last too long, and I was on my way to checkout, having no idea if I'd insulted my friend's friend or not. It was just another in a series of interactions that I and other hearing-impaired people have to manage.

At the Home Depot, as in all retail interactions, I reached another decision point when the self-checkout lines were full.

A helpful employee moved behind a register, looked in my direction, and said something. Given the context, it was almost certainly, "I can help you here," but between the mask and the Plexiglas divider, she could have been telling me my hair was on fire.

And, just like that, the next daily adventure in profound hearing loss was underway. At that moment, a song popped into my head, "Once in a Lifetime" by Talking Heads. I was never into eighties new wave, but one lyric jumped out: *"How did I get here?"*

For most of my life, I thought everyone heard in bits and pieces, sounds coming and going like a fleeting thought, almost there, and then gone. As far back as I can remember, I caught sounds in clips—kids in school telling stories and laughing, my mom and dad asking something that didn't quite make sense. Without realizing it, I inched closer or moved in front to hear and see what was being said. Lipreading, it turns out, is an instinct you pick up long before you know it's needed. My teachers often said things that didn't make sense. Why did Chicago have the world's air? And how exactly did green plants eat photos and incense? It took weeks for me to realize that Chicago hosted the World's Fair, and plants conduct photosynthesis, a word that was much easier to read than hear. I was an active participant in all these clues, constantly working to put the puzzle pieces together. As Sir Paul and Mr. Lennon kept telling me, *"Think of what you're saying / You can get it wrong and still you think that it's all right / We can work it out / We can work it out."*

At the time, like all kids, I had no idea this process was unique to me. I felt like life couldn't get better, especially around the time of second grade. For starters, I was slightly ahead of everyone else in Mrs. Kline's classroom when it came to my addition tables. I could breeze through the nines while everyone else struggled. *Nine plus five is fourteen. Nine plus six is fifteen.* I could see the logic. It was like adding ten and taking one away. Why other kids couldn't get that was beyond me, but I loved it. I could see the other kids frantically counting on their fingers, which made me smile. Competition and goal setting came naturally. I just didn't realize what they were called at the time.

Second grade was also my first exposure to the "cool" I'd seen in shows like *The A-Team* and *The Fall Guy*. I'd been moved to the back row. Mrs. Kline thought I was an overzealous hand-raiser, and she didn't want me distracting other kids. At first, I thought this was punishment. I had no idea that being in the back row was like a bad-boy badge of honor. The only things missing were a leather jacket and biker boots. I even got the coolest outlaw desk in the school. Newburgh, my town in Indiana, had experienced a population surge that required the elementary school to pull in some additional desks from high school storage. All the "kid" desks matched: manila-colored plastic tops with a slate-gray cubby underneath and adjustable steel legs. But the back row, the badlands, had wooden-topped desks with rusty racks underneath, big enough for actual books. None of the nuts and bolts matched. Basically, the eight-year-old's version of a T-top Trans Am.

As if life needed to get cooler, some long-gone high schooler, a kid who must have hitchhiked to California by now, had carved a message into the wood that read: "Pantera Rocks Ass." I had no idea who or what a Pantera was, nor did I have any idea what rocking ass meant. But I knew that I had lucked out. Steppenwolf's "Born to Be Wild" had to be playing somewhere. Life couldn't get any better.

Then Nurse Diane wheeled in her dreaded cart, and things changed.

Every year, the school nurse, known by everyone as Nurse Diane, visited classrooms with her audio laboratory on wheels. It was armed with a power strip and a couple of ancient devices covered with metal switches and various knobs. Out of that entanglement came a set of wire-framed headphones, large and bulky, that connected to her tabletop devices with a garden-hose-sized cable.

The headphones, far too large for my fifty-five-pound frame, clamped on like alligator bites. They were supposed to deliver various tones to measure hearing sensitivity at different volumes and pitches. But when I put them on, the headphones didn't seem to work. They only played the loud and low tones, ones I could feel more than hear.

Today, medical testing is done in private, if performed in a school setting at all. But in 1985 no one seemed concerned with patient privacy. Hearing tests were performed at the teacher's desk, front and center. One by one, each of my friends took their spots in the same creaky wooden chair. They pried apart the headphones and winced as they clamped on their ears. Nurse Diane then fumbled with some switches and knobs as I watched with rapt attention. That was followed by my classmates raising their hands. The same process went on all morning. Nurse Diane moved her hands around on her contraption and a kid's hand would shoot up as if he had to go the bathroom.

When it was time for the back row, I'd been watching for what seemed like hours. Through instinct, I had calibrated how often my classmates had raised their hands and how much spacing came between the lifts. *Nurse moves her hand over the device, a few seconds later an arm goes up, got it.* No second grader realizes that he's learning pattern identification, but most kids don't realize they're losing their hearing, either.

When my turn came, I took my seat, stuck my head in the earphone vise and waited. The nurse conducted her orchestra of buttons and dials.

I heard a low, tuba tone, about the consistency of a tugboat horn. Or maybe I felt it in my chest. Either way, my arm shot up.

Then I heard an equally loud but slightly higher trombone tone. These were easy. My arm shot up again.

The next sound was a clarinet, the same note as the tugboat and the trombone but a couple of octaves higher. My hand fired skyward. I was rocking ass like Pantera, whatever that meant.

Then came a higher tone, quieter, but I still heard it, or thought I did. My arm went up again, but with a tentative air.

After that, nothing. Sound vanished. I saw Nurse Diane continue her symphony of movement, so I rested the requisite number of beats and then raised my hand as before. Maybe the headphones were broken. Out of the corner of my eye, I caught Nurse Diane nod ever so slightly, a subconscious acknowledgment that my guesses were paying off. We danced our silent little samba for a few more minutes. Then the nurse motioned for me to take off the headphones.

"Are you feeling okay today, Matt?" she asked loudly enough for all my friends to hear. That question hadn't been asked of the other kids.

"I feel fine," I said, wounded that I had been singled out. I waited for the next question, with an eight-year-old ego to protect. But there wasn't another question. Like any elementary school medical professional, Nurse Diane nodded and said, "Okay, next."

My back-row-rebel life didn't last long. Like most children, I compensated for my deficiencies without realizing it. The next time the seating chart was updated, I crept closer to the front, not because I wanted to ingratiate myself with my teacher, but because I felt left out by not hearing, even though I didn't consciously know it. The desire to fit in is overwhelming, and not just in preteen boys, so I inched forward, first to the center, then closer to the front. From up there, I could turn around and see a friend's lips move. As a bonus, I could follow what the teacher said.

In third grade and then fourth, the nurse rolled the cart in again for the ritual. There was no rhyme or reason to the timing. We might be in the middle of circling nouns and underlining verbs when the class door would creak open. As always, I took my turn in the chair, fumbling with the headphones, trying my best to look cool and in charge. The beeps grew fainter each year. I assumed that was part of the test. Every subject in school got tougher as you got older. Why should a hearing test be different? And, as always, it didn't take long for the sounds to stop. As I had learned to do in the second grade, I studied the nurse's cues and raised my hand when I thought there should be tones, even though I heard nothing. I felt like I was playing that game where you put your hands atop another person's and try to pull them away before they can slap you on the knuckles. Losing my hearing wasn't even a thought. I just didn't want to stand out in front of Jill Tuley, my elementary school crush.

As part of what was now a standard practice, the nurse asked me if I was feeling okay. She didn't frown, but I could see wrinkles form between her eyebrows. The muscles around her upper lip tightened. Picking up on nonverbal cues is another instinct that accelerates when you don't hear well. This all happened decades ago, but I still remember the feeling I had when the nurse came in with the cart. Other kids were thrilled at the prospect of putting the math books away while they listened to beeps. I always felt a wilting mortification, the dread that comes from being young and under a spotlight, fearful that you've failed without knowing the benchmark for success. I always aimed to please. The looks of concern I often got told me that I'd somehow missed. The only thing worse than being a young boy screwing up in school is having no idea what you've done wrong.

Then, one afternoon, out of the blue, I got into my mom's car and, as usual, she asked how my day went. Good. It was good. Monosyllabic answers are often a man's best friend.

Then she said, "Are you feeling okay?"

By then the question was getting old. I said I felt fine.

Then she asked something that threw me off. "Matt, you can hear me okay, can't you?"

"Yeah, Mom," I said. "I hear you okay."

She nodded and gave a hint of a smile. That was it. No more discussion. Riding home, I stared at the passing houses in our town, a cloudless Midwestern sky running away to the edge of nowhere. Of course, I heard okay.

At that moment, through the speakers of Mom's baby-blue Dodge Caravan, I could hear Don Henley. The words were as crisp as the fall air. *"A little voice inside my head said, 'Don't look back, you can never look back.'"*

TWO

HEAR MY WORDS THAT I MIGHT TEACH YOU

—Paul Simon

ENIAL ISN'T A CONSCIOUS CHOICE. Nobody wakes up one morning and decides to believe the sky is green or the earth is flat. It comes slowly and with a hint of seduction at each decision point. All humans tend to ignore evidence that will lead to outcomes we don't like. History books are filled with examples, big and small. But whether it's an entire continent pretending the rise of a murderous tyrant isn't real or a friend eating one, then two, then three packets of Tums a day and thinking everything is normal until he's rushed to the hospital for an emergency appendectomy, it's always easier to see the obvious when you're not the one being seduced. When it is you who, for example, needs the volume up to 10, 12, 15, and then 20 to hear the dialogue of a movie, you rationalize the problem away. The television is getting older, or maybe this part is supposed to be soft. Denial has a closet filled with costumes, all distracting and seemingly new.

The Indiana of my childhood was exactly what you'd expect. Neighbors knew each other and everyone was aware of everyone else's business. Kids started work the second they were old enough, and a lot of them raced go-karts after school long before they had driver's licenses. Depending on the season, the biggest events of the weekends were high school football and basketball games followed by pizza at Mazzio's. Church on Sunday came up next. Few residents of the town missed any of it. Those who didn't own pickup trucks either used to or wished they did. But no matter what you drove, there were plenty of spots where you could ride for miles and see nothing but flat soybean fields and an occasional corn crop, with the odd grain silo jutting up like a giant thumb. Even so, people felt close to each other in a way that made you certain the friendships you made would last forever. It was like *The Wonder Years* but with Madonna as a backstory instead of Vietnam.

Hoosiers, at least the ones I knew, also loved the outdoors. When I was young, there was a family that had one of those old-time dinner bells like you've seen in western movies. It was mounted on a pole at the top of their driveway. The mother would ring it when she wanted the kids to come home. You could hear it for half a mile, at least. Nobody thought that was unusual. In the pre-cell-phone era, it was ingenious. Whether it was biking, hiking, fishing, or just hanging out with friends under the stars, time slipped by in my town. It was good to have a bell to remind you when to go home.

We were solidly Midwestern and middle class. My parents worked in the school system, so material wealth was always out of the question, even though we always had everything we needed. Dad taught middle school shop, which meant he had summers off. With that extra time, he and I, along with my older brother, did what we broadly described as "outside work," which included trimming and removing trees, uprooting old shrubbery, blasting stumps with questionable demolition techniques, painting houses, and cutting firewood. This was all part of a typical June in my childhood. I also mowed lawns from the time I was old enough to pull the starter rope on a two-cycle engine. The bark of a lawn mower and the incessant whine of a trimmer were rites of passage. I cannot remember a time when I was not around screeching chain saws. When I got old enough to hold one, Dad taught me how to respect and use it, gripping firmly but never forcing the teeth into the skin of a tree, always being aware that this was a dangerous machine that could kick back and cut off an arm. What we never talked about was the effect on hearing. Caring for my ears wasn't yet a part of my life but I know now a good rule of thumb is that if a person standing three feet away can't hear you when you yell, you're probably damaging your auditory receptors.

Some of my strongest memories growing up involved the squall of a Stihl 170 and the smell and taste of fresh sawdust. The felling of a tree always brought sunlight, a sense of accomplishment, and a high-pitched ringing in the back of my skull that lasted at least a couple of hours. I always felt close to manhood when another truck bed was loaded with the proof of our labors. There was something about cutting wood that made a boy feel like he'd crossed a bridge to another phase of life; something that connected every male to his ancestors going back to the dawn of civilization. After loading the truck with the remnants of a tree, we would pile into the cab, and I would stare out the window as the twelve-string backbeat of Gordon Lightfoot in C major, three-quarter time, poured out of the speakers. *"The legend lives on from the Chippewa on down / Of the big lake they call Gitchee Gumee . . ."*

As I got a little older, "The Wreck of the Edmund Fitzgerald" hit me a lot harder than it did when I was a kid, not because I could relate to shipwrecks or *"hurricane west winds,"* but instead because I knew what it felt like to be swallowed by forces beyond my control. I understood the question, *"Does anyone know where the love of God goes / When the waves turn the minutes to hours?"*

As a kid, though, I felt as invincible as most. I shot rifles, shotguns, and pistols in my downtime, often at cans or bottles, and almost never while wearing enough ear protection. We also went to tractor pulls and monster truck rallies, which had the best lemonade stands I've ever found. I was almost always near the front, where the dirt and dust would settle on my clothes and in my eyes, and the thunderous roars of the machines hit me in the chest like a giant open hand. As a result, I barely noticed when the upper registers of sound disappeared entirely. And I didn't pay attention when the euphemism "hard of hearing" became "can't hear certain sounds at all."

Like all evolving humans, I adapted. My gradual hearing loss inadvertently led to me becoming a better student and leader. I moved up to the front of the class and paid closer attention because I had to. I couldn't hear what was going on otherwise. I also made the subconscious choice to speak up more often. If I could control situations, I could steer dialogue. And if I took charge of what was being discussed, I had a better chance of figuring out what was being said.

Also, as long as you are speaking you don't have to listen. Most people consider that narcissism and a bad look. For centuries, moms around the world have uttered some variation of "God gave you one mouth and two ears for a reason." But in high school, confidence is currency. If you're a natural conversationalist, you have a better shot at being accepted in different circles. Teens often divide into two groups: those who are comfortable with who they are and those who pretend to be. I chose the latter, putting on the best fake-it-till-you-make-it disguise in school. Then I went to work developing friendships with people I saw lifting others up, hoping they'd do the same for me. Finding that support was an early coping mechanism, although at the time I just wanted people to laugh with over a slice of pizza. Just as controlling a conversation meant I had a better chance at understanding things, so did controlling my environment. I went so far as to run for class president so I could be involved in deciding when, where, and how social events occurred. There was no underlying agenda, at least not a conscious one, but being in control of certain things did allow me to construct an environment where I fit. I won the election, although, I'll just admit it, I ran unopposed, and will be remembered by my classmates, if at all, as the president who made the lights at the school dances too bright.

There were also forgettable athletic endeavors. I ran track, slowly. I played baseball and soccer, rising to the level of mediocre. I dated a wonderful girl. The class president gig came with a front-row parking spot, which I relished. I cruised our town with my friends singing along with Snoop: *"Rollin' down the street, smokin' indo / Sippin' on gin and juice, laid back,"* each of us wondering if we were alone in having no idea what any of that meant. My friends knew that I was hard of hearing. That was impossible to hide, especially given how I had to lean forward and say, "What was that?" But it was not a big deal for anyone—right up until the moment that it was.

By my junior year of high school, I was taking a lot of advanced placement courses, because my much smarter friends were taking those classes and I wanted to hang out with them all day. The possibility of also getting into a better-than-average college was a by-product that I was willing to accept. As I did with most things, I made a list of colleges, one I had written out and meticulously considered, by which I mean, I laid out the brochures and chose the ones that looked the coolest. My college choices based on that criterion were the University of Colorado in Boulder, the brochure of which left me wide-eyed and anxious; the University of Michigan, where I knew I would have a great time attending Big Ten football games; and the United States Military Academy at West Point, most commonly known as Army, the place from which Ulysses S. Grant, Dwight Eisenhower, John J. Pershing, and Douglas MacArthur graduated, and where George Armstrong Custer (class of 1861) is buried.

Because things were generally easy for me, I fell into the habit of sliding through life with as little effort as possible, doing the minimum to make the desired grade. My parents recognized this and made subtle efforts to express their disapproval by saying things like "We're tired of you constantly doing just enough to get by." I read between the lines, even though I failed to comprehend why anyone would waste time trying to make a better grade than a low A. If it rounded up to an A, it was the same grade as the kid who made a hundred.

Mom and Dad's reminders about my effort didn't take hold nearly as well as the brochures from Uncle Sam. West Point, on paper, challenged me with concepts like Duty, Honor, Discipline, and Service. Those were the core principles at Army. And they were exactly the kind of challenge I needed.

My mom and I met with a friend and her son who had finished his second year at West Point. Over chicken fingers, I tried not to let the awe I felt for this guy across from me show. Not only was he a future second lieutenant in the world's greatest army, he was also a Division I distance swimmer, a soldier with a Speedo.

"My mom says you're interested in West Point?" he said to me after we placed our orders at the local chicken-finger restaurant.

This would be the first chance I'd ever have to get a first-person account of the place, so I had carefully prepared a response.

"Yeah," I confirmed.

"Cool, but yeah, man." He looked over to see if the moms were listening. Seeing that they were engrossed in their own conversations, he added, "I wouldn't do it."

That was unexpected. "Why did you go?" I asked.

"I loved the challenge of competitive swimming and wanted to swim in college. West Point gave me the chance."

"It's great that you get to do that, though, right?"

"I guess, but now swimming at, like, four each morning is the only easy part of my day."

That wasn't in the brochure. It was also the kind of challenge that excited me. I ignored the warnings of the swimmer. I wanted an atypical college experience, a challenge that would push me to my fullest. Swimming at 4:00 A.M. was never going to happen, but I wanted to do hard things, to accomplish more before breakfast than my high school classmates would all day. My goal was an appointment to the most elite military institute in the world.

The campus at West Point sits on the spot where General George Washington strung a giant chain across a bend at the "west point" in the Hudson River to block British warships on their way to New York. From the steep hills on either side of the river, Washington's Continental Army blasted the ships and created quite a mess. A link of that giant chain is on display at the West Point campus.

Those stories would captivate any eighteen-year-old. But I

also loved the idea of being an army officer. Plus, it was free, which was not a small thing for my family. Even though we could afford some tuition, there would be a lot of satisfaction in telling Dad that the cost was covered. Once you are accepted as a cadet, you show up on R day, the first day of training for incoming candidates, with nothing more than a toothbrush and underwear. Everything else is provided, including one of the best educations in the world.

As a bonus, when executive search firms list the top schools that their placements have come from, the Army, Navy, and Air Force academies are always one, two, and three. Those graduates have not only gone through extensive leadership training and rigorous academic work; they've also spent a minimum of five years as military officers. That's the deal. The United States government pays for your education and training, about a million dollars in real costs, and you agree to serve your country in uniform for at least five years. Not only is your education free, but you are guaranteed a job with a lot of responsibility when you graduate.

Those were the practical reasons for wanting to go to West Point. But there was also an emotional component. Anyone who chooses to attend a service academy does so for a higher purpose. You understand that you give up the college parties on Friday nights and the morning conversations at the coffee shops; you don't get to grow your hair and wear sweatpants and flip-flops to class; you forgo fraternity rituals and sorority socials for daily barrack inspections, mountain training, fast roping, small-arms engagement, and urban assault tactics. As a high school senior, you make that choice because you want to be a part of something bigger than yourself; something noble. You want to serve a country and a cause.

My dad and I spent a lot of time together, but rarely over sports. His love language was sharing his passion for hard work, along with some hunting and fishing. That's why the rare football game we watched together stood out. It was always played in early December: the Army-Navy game. Dad was not a military man. West Point wasn't a legacy thing for me. But the few times we watched the Army-Navy game, neither of us said much, which was unusual for my dad, who was a natural-born storyteller. He told the same stories so often that we finally told him he should number them. That way, rather than take the time to tell the whole thing, he could just say, "Number eight," and we'd all laugh. But there was a lot of reverent silence during the Army-Navy game. The scenes said it all. The entire student bodies from both schools marched onto the field in dress uniform and stood in formation. Then they filed into the stands, where they all stood for the entire game. The president usually attended. Sometimes he flipped the coin. It was a sporting spectacle unlike any other because of what those men on the field do after graduation.

I threw myself into studying and training for a West Point appointment. I had all the paperwork lined up, all the essays written, and all the recommendations in place, including one from our congressman, Frank McCloskey. I was ready to go.

The only thing left was a standard army physical. Our family practitioner wouldn't do. Dad and I had to drive three hundred miles to Fort Knox, Kentucky. The entire way, we listened to *Bob Dylan's Greatest Hits* and Simon and Garfunkel's *The Concert in Central Park*. Dad didn't talk much on that drive. He'd grown up in the Vietnam era. As a concept, he supported the armed forces. But the practical notion of his son in uniform, perhaps leading an infantry platoon in some faraway land, left him a little melancholy. Watching him mouth the words *"Your sons and your daughters / Are beyond your command / Your old road is rapidly agin',"* I wondered if Dad was singing or trying to convince himself.

The physical I took was, to be charitable, thorough. A polished and no-nonsense army doctor went through all the expected tests and a few that were a surprise. When we left Fort Knox, I thought my career path was set. My friends knew that I was bound for New York with a gray uniform and crew cut.

Then the envelope arrived. I almost didn't notice the word "FAILED" at the top. I'd assumed this was just a formality. I was healthier than most kids my age. I wasn't overweight, I ate well, and I had been running and working out to get ready for plebe year. I did a double take and read it two, three, and four times to make sure I understood.

FAILED. **Substandard Auditory Acuity.**

All rejections are tough, and I had been through a few already, a hard no when I asked a girl on a date and a soft one when I wanted to take the car to a party. This was the first one that I knew had life-altering consequences. Like all eighteen-year-old males, I had to register for the draft. Here I was trying to volunteer, attempting to be all I could be, and the United States Army was telling me that I wasn't healthy enough. Just like that, a dream crashed hard. That pain, sharp and piercing, hot and electric, kept me hunched over for days.

Like the heartbreak that comes after first love, I thought this agony was permanent, a new condition of life. The contractions in my gut felt like a creature tearing me open from the inside out. From that moment forward, I knew that I would be known by everyone as a failure, a "substandard" who wasn't good enough to serve in uniform. I felt broken. Even more important, I was stranded, adrift without a rudder or a sail, a class officer with high grades and a solid résumé, but no college, all because I was "hard of hearing," a euphemism for "second rate," like "a little slow" or "his daddy drinks."

My family is Protestant, which means I grew up going to a church that hammered home the belief that God had a plan, and whether or not we liked the steps along the way, every life was created for a reason. Mom and Dad reinforced that message after the disappointment of West Point. There was probably an anecdote about one set of footprints in the sand, or perhaps a parable about a door closing so others could open. I wanted none of it. In my eighteen-year-old mind, all I could process was the fact that I had been invincible when I woke up the morning of the physical, and now I was going to bed every night physically unfit to serve my country.

Everyone tried to buck me up. The West Point life wasn't for me, they said. I would have hated it. Don't listen to them. You're fine. That kind of support eased the vise a little. Still, even though the word was already forbidden in polite company, I felt like an emotional cripple for a while.

My parents came to the rescue. Mom informed me that because of my dad's joy in frugality, they had been able to put my brother through Purdue University debt-free. They could do the same for me, so long as I chose an in-state school. So the mountains of Boulder and the football Saturdays of Ann Arbor were tossed in the trash can. I applied and was accepted into Indiana University. It proved to be the best move of my life. Turned out the closed door did, indeed, open another.

I fell into a major in marketing. I joined a fraternity. And since I was a nineteen-year-old male, I pushed my hearing loss off to the side, as if none of the warning signs had ever appeared. When I couldn't hear a professor in a large lecture auditorium, I blamed it on the acoustics. Napping on the couches with the Notorious B.I.G. or 2Pac blaring over the knee-high speakers while a couple of guys argued about East Coast versus West Coast rap never fazed me. Many times, I heard "Dude, I can't believe you slept through that," which often came across as, *"Doo . . . ca-tee ept . . . at."* It didn't dawn on me that this was unusual. Sound sleeping had always been an asset, or so I thought.

It was a telephone that jolted me back to reality. Back in the days when landlines were still a thing, our fraternity house had a communal phone in the hallway. I noticed that the ringer kept getting turned down to the point where I could barely hear it. Only when I checked, the ringer was at full volume. It's one thing to assume a lecture auditorium has bad acoustics or that you're able to sleep through parties because you're a sound sleeper. But when a hammer striking a bell gets progressively quieter over a short period of time, even an egocentric college sophomore can figure out that the problem might be him.

Indiana University Medical Center is top shelf. As a student, I had access to free routine checkups. It wasn't as if I was uninsured or would struggle with a copay. I had, by that point, taken and failed plenty of hearing tests, so I had a good baseline of knowledge going in. What I did not expect was the look of concern on the audiologist's face as he said, "I think we need to get you in for an MRI."

That had never happened before. So, I went back later and lay on a cold hard table that slid into a tube about the size of a coffin. Then came the bangs, rapid fire, like a Gatling gun. I understood the concept of magnetic resonance imaging, but I'd never heard about the noise.

I guess I should have been happy I could hear it, because a few days later, I got a call from IU Health. "You have bilateral acoustic neuromas," the matter-of-fact internist informed me. Knowing that I had no idea what that meant, he added, "tumors on the hearing nerves of your brain."

Even though I wasn't completely deaf at that time, I didn't hear a lot after that. The words "tumors" and "brain" in the same sentence hit you like a board. It's hard to pay attention to anything after that opener. I certainly didn't hear the words "brain surgery," although they were, in fact, uttered. I would need surgery, and not in some long-distant future. Little did I know, but the surgery would be the first of many. I also could never have imagined how everything in my life would change after that. What if I had been at West Point? Would this have been discovered sooner? Later? At all? What if I had been way out in Colorado, not close enough to home to call my parents and have them drive up at a moment's notice?

Indiana was where I was supposed to be, and not just for my initial diagnosis. Something even more substantive and lasting would happen there. College at IU was where I would meet Nora, who would coauthor the soundtrack of my life from that moment forward.

THREE

MEDICINE HAS COME A LONG WAY IN THE LAST THIRTY YEARS. As recently as 1993, only about 5 percent of newborns were tested for hearing loss before leaving the hospital. Now, it is almost universal. Parents have to opt out of the test, and very few do. North of 97 percent of newborns have hearing tests within the first couple of days of life. The reason for that dramatic shift is the knowledge of what's possible through early detection. Many cognitive pathways that permanently affect speech and overall development are formed between birth and age three. Early detection leads to early treatment. That's why you see a lot more kids with hearing aids today than you did thirty or forty years ago.

We also have mainstreamed genetic testing. While there are a lot of bioethical implications, parents can know a lot about their child's genetic predispositions early, and sometimes before they're born. That knowledge, if you choose to obtain it, allows you to prepare for some of the hurdles life invariably sets in your way.

On the other end of the age spectrum, only about 7 percent of the people in their fifties who suffer from hearing loss get treatment, including hearing aids. That number goes up to about 17 percent of people in their seventies who need auditory assistance. Even though more senior citizens get hearing aids when they need them, the numbers are still low. You would expect older people to accept the reality of hearing loss and take advantage of available technology. But a majority who need help don't get it. That is partly because of the cost, partly because of vanity, partly out of an aversion to technology or a hesitancy to change. Whatever the reason, almost 80 percent of seventy-something-year-olds who need hearing aids don't get them.

As big a problem as that might be, there is another swath of the population for which almost no data is available: people who experience hearing loss sometime between their first day of kindergarten and their fiftieth birthday. That's a lot of people who, for years, have been stranded on an island. A lot happens in that stretch of life. It would be nice to know your options.

Those were among the myriad thoughts I had as I read everything that I could on neurofibromatosis type 2, commonly referred to as NF2, the diagnosis I received from a team of specialists not long after my initial call from the IU

Medical Center. I learned, for starters, that my condition was genetic and relatively rare. I didn't catch a virus or develop some disorder. Sometimes NF2 is passed down from parents to children and other times it pops up spontaneously. Either way, it's caused by a defect in the gene that gives rise to something called schwannomin, a structural protein located on chromosome 22. The result of this defect is noncancerous tumors on the brain, spinal cord, and peripheral nerves, most prevalently, cranial nerve VIII, which is the auditory vestibular nerve.

That is a complicated way of saying that there was corrosive buildup on the wiring between my ears and my brain. It's also a great opportunity to darkly joke that "NF tumors get on my nerves." The ears themselves, all the tiny bones and hair follicles that receive and filter sound, appeared to work fine. My eardrum vibrated just as well as anyone else's. The blockage occurred in the nerves that transmitted that sound to my brain.

At first, I thought this was good news. Now that we had the problem isolated, doctors could remove the tumors and I would be ready to go; like splicing a broken wire, voilà, everything's fine. I pitched that hypothesis to my doctors, who were kind enough not to laugh out loud at me. Unfortunately, as I was quickly informed, nerves in your brain are different from wires in your car. You can't replace them or cut out the bad parts and bind the two ends together with electrical tape. Taking out my tumors was, to be literal, brain surgery. And the nerves in that area of the body don't respond well to scalpels. Surgeons needed to cut out the tumors, but no one was sure what the resulting damage would be.

Then there was the source problem. Even if I made it through this cutting process without any damage, I still had the gene defect, which meant more tumors were coming in the future. We could be stuck on repeat for quite some time.

As depressing as that realization was, things got worse. The specialists informed me that, even with this surgery and others I would need in the future, I was eventually going to be deaf: not "hard of hearing," not "crank up the volume another notch or two," but stone-deaf. Medical experts could slow the process through treatment, but one day I would wake up and hear nothing at all.

Hearing that news was like being hit between the eyes with a hammer. My mother's soft hum; my father's stories, the ones stuck on repeat; my fraternity brothers' bad jokes; the throaty roar of a fast car; the ticking of a clock; the steady rumble of a train: all of it would be gone. And the music. Did this mean I would never hear Paul and Artie's tight harmonies as they ran through the spice rack of "Scarborough Fair"? *"Hello, darkness, my old friend,"* indeed.

Sometimes anguish comes ahead of the loss. When I learned that deafness was a foregone conclusion, at first, I panicked. How would I hear a smoke alarm? Can deaf people still drive even though they can't hear horns, or trucks, or train whistles? In that moment, those concerns were years away, but the brain tends to race when processing bad news. I also went through all the stages of grief. Some people say there are five; others say seven. I didn't count. At first, I didn't believe the doctors. They had to be wrong. I was healthy in every other way. According to the materials I could find on NF2, balance should have been a problem. I also read where you got cataracts in your eyes, and there were skin lesions. I had none of that. The diagnosis had to be wrong.

The doctors nodded. They had heard all this before. Yes, sometimes there were other symptoms, some quite severe, but the most common was a progressive loss of hearing. My case, they assured me, was textbook NF2.

That news led to hurt—not an emotional pain like breaking up with a girlfriend, but a deep, raw burn in my gut coupled with a sharp, steady throb that ran up my neck and into the base of my skull. I also felt guilty for all the times I had ignored my bad hearing. I felt silly for all the excuses I'd made. Of course, the speakers in the car were fine. Yes, the acoustics of the room were normal. No, your friends weren't whispering just to annoy you. I was becoming deaf the whole time. What an idiot I had been to think otherwise.

After my diagnosis, and after processing the implications as thoroughly as possible, I returned to Indiana University for my junior year and tried to pretend that nothing had changed. Learning that you will eventually go deaf is, to some degree, the same mental process that people go through with any awful and irreversible diagnosis. I don't have MS or ALS or any of the multitude of heartbreaking diseases that rack lives and strain relationships, but I know what it feels like to know something bad is on the way. It's like waiting for a steamroller to mow you down. Even though you know it's coming, the machine is a long way off, and steamrollers are slow. In the beginning, that makes the anxiety unbearable. Then, eventually, you look up and see the steamroller, knowing it's still coming, but you don't think about it afterward.

I shared my diagnosis with a few friends, especially my fraternity brothers, who had helped me navigate the transitional waters of adulthood since I had arrived on campus as a wide-eyed freshman. I also had a job in the IU Athletic Department, so it was imperative that I share my new diagnosis with an adviser there. "Oh," he said. "My dad's the head of the Speech and Hearing Department. You should go see him."

Armed with a recommendation and feeling pretty down, I did something uncommon for me at the time: I acted on the offer and trekked to the other side of campus to the IU Heath and Sciences building to see my adviser's father. That walk couldn't have taken more than twenty minutes, even though I tend to stroll and get distracted by passersby, but it was like moving from Bloomington to Botswana. The Indiana campus was not officially divided into two halves, but there was certainly a sense of demarcation between east and west. While both are beautiful, the west side of campus, where I spent nearly all of my time, was filled with kids in Birkenstocks and khakis named Hannah and Trent, walking through tulip gardens on their way to or from a marketing or communications class. Everyone smiled, because they felt secure in their future prospects, even though few of them ever took a test with an objectively wrong answer.

East campus was where the science and math students poured out of the library like walking zombies. They were the students who had pulled all-nighters studying for chemistry or advanced biology classes that most definitely had right and wrong answers. When I made my way over, I might have been the only person with combed hair. Everyone else on that side of campus seemed sidetracked by things like academic effort. At first, I observed my surroundings like a tourist in some far-distant land. Then I remembered that I was there in the hopes that one of those science types could help me. I soldiered on until I found the old limestone building where I bounded downstairs to the basement to meet the man I'd come to see: Dr. Hipskind.

I always assumed that auditory departments wound up in basements because of some health-care hierarchy. Neurology shared the top floor with cancer study, followed one floor below by heart disease. The hearing doctors were relegated to the basement. Of course, that was wrong. Audiology specialists preferred basements because underground floors are quieter. Hearing tests can be conducted without a lot of ambient noise from the street or sidewalk. Also, those professional audiology booths, the ones that look like bank vaults, are heavy. Gravity remains undefeated, so getting the materials for those booths down is a lot easier than hoisting them up.

Dr. Hipskind put me at ease. Part of it was the shock of white hair that gave him an Albert Einstein look, but he also knew how to talk to people with hearing loss. Eye contact, simple sentences, and consistently asking "Did I explain that well?" That last question proved to be the most powerful, because it took the responsibility of misunderstanding off me and my faulty ears, and placed it onto him, the speaker. It was early in the process, but I was learning that doctors sometimes have two communication modes: science-speak, which only they understand, or unintentional condescension, the "there, there, let me put this in itsy-bitsy, unscary words so you get it" language you might use if speaking to a kindergarten class or a pet corgi. Dr. Hipskind struck the right balance of man-to-man conversation with doctor-patient understanding. He also projected a brilliant grandpa vibe, a caring genius who would first do no harm. I had brought a mountain of paperwork from all the tests and treatments I had received, including my NF2 diagnosis. Rather than look at any of it, Dr. Hipskind said, "Why don't we start anew."

He proposed that in exchange for premium quality hearing aids and full hearing care on campus, I would become a class guinea pig for graduate students in his audiology program. They could practice their hearing evaluation and diagnostic skills on a patient who wasn't faking it. They could also work on fitting hearing aids and on their bedside manner with a patient who couldn't hear a car horn from thirty yards away. I wasn't sure how much of the treatment Dr. Hipskind proposed would have been covered under my parents' insurance anyway, but I did know that Dad couldn't have been happier that I saved him a few bucks.

I quickly signed on and set a schedule to be Dr. Hipskind's lab rat. However, I was also an evaluator, part of the teaching process, which made the experience fun. As a grizzled veteran of the hearing-test game, the judgments I passed on the grad students were fair but hard. It didn't take long to figure out which students knew what they were doing and which ones were trying to tap-dance their way through. They were taking a test for which I had the answer key memorized. A dozen students tested my hearing with varying degrees of success.

After that, I moved to what looked like a dental chair for

a new experiment. The first time, students on each side filled my ears with an expanding foam that looked like caulk. Only about a third of the substance went into my ears. The rest ballooned out like two softballs on the sides of my head.

When Dr. Hipskind came in to inspect the class, he smiled and shook his head. "Why don't I give this a go," he said. He took the caulk guns and filled my ears with a small amount of the expandable substance. After a couple of minutes, he took out the molds, held them up for the class and said, "See."

The molds were sent to a hearing aid company, and about a week later I got a call asking me to come in to have the devices fitted and installed. With the caulk molds having covered every nook and cranny of my ears, the hearing aids fit like a second skin. These were the first digital aids I had ever seen—cutting-edge technology at the time, and something I couldn't have afforded without Dr. Hipskind's help.

The devices were turned on, and while I couldn't tell much of a difference in the basement, the second I stepped outside I felt like I'd been dropped in a noise machine. A rush of sounds hit me from every direction. At first, I heard a loud bang that I thought was a gunshot. It turned out to be the door of the office slamming behind me. Then I heard birds chirping, kids talking, bike tires humming against the sidewalk. I heard cars passing, a breeze rustling the leaves in the trees. I felt like Superman when he first tries to harness his super hearing. Everything hit me at once. After a moment of discriminating among different sounds, I heard an odd whoosh, whoosh, whoosh that I couldn't identify. I looked around and saw nothing, but the sound continued—whoosh, whoosh, whoosh.

I was almost on the other side of campus before I realized that it was the inseams of my Levi's rubbing against each other with each step I took.

For several months, as I continued to be Dr. Hipskind's pet subject, I thought I might have found the answer. Those other doctors had to be wrong. No way I was going deaf with this kind of progress. Unfortunately, it didn't take long for the hearing aids to stop picking up the sounds they had on that first day. Where I had initially been able to hear a song on a stereo from a dorm window across the street—*"Do you remember / The twenty-first night of September? / Love was changing the minds of pretenders"*—now I couldn't hear someone calling my name from across a hall.

People on the outside view hearing loss as a constant downward plunge on a graph. You hear fine one day, and the next day it's a little worse, followed by a steady decline until you wake up one morning and the world is silent. That's not how it works. Instead of a plunging line on a graph, hearing loss is like a roller coaster. You get hearing aids, and you start the slow, upward incline—clack, clack, clack—as your brain adjusts to sounds you had forgotten existed. The more adjustments, the higher the hill gets. But eventually hearing loss outraces technology, you crest the hill, and you leave your seat as you plunge downward. The descent is always faster. Then some new technology comes along. You level out and start another slow climb. The thrill of going up causes you to relax and take a breath, maybe look around at the view. But you know what's coming. You've been on this ride before. You can feel the incline reaching its peak. Rather than checking out the rest of the park—oh, look, there's the haunted house over by the carousel—or looking at the city skyline in the distance, you grab on to the safety bar and pull it a little tighter over your thighs. Once you start downhill again, your sight narrows and your focus shifts. You are only looking at the track ahead, wondering how low you will go this time. My first time hearing the classic "Helter Skelter" was on U2's *Rattle & Hum* live album. I didn't know the full history, but Bono kicked it off by noting that it was a song Charles Manson stole from the Beatles. Bono said he was stealing it back. That intro, followed by the opening lyrics, *"When I get to the bottom, I go back to the top of the slide / Where I stop and I turn and I go for a ride / Till I get to the bottom and I see you again,"* always felt chaotic to me even in middle school. I never expected to so closely relate so deeply to a song about having something taken away, trying to get it back, and the ups and downs of the ride along the way.

Over the years my hearing aids got bigger and stronger. The digital tech improved and the technicians got better at adjusting to my specific needs. But the hill was always going to crest. Free fall was inevitable, until the day came when the ride would stop.

Dr. Hipskind could not have been more forthright. He could help. Adjusting the hearing aids, making them stronger and fine-tuning them for my specific audiological needs, would help for a while, years perhaps, but I should not get my hopes up. My diagnosis had a predictable outcome. I would one day lose my hearing entirely. The steamroller was coming, slow and steady, but still en route.

That turned out to be the good news. Other outcomes from NF2 were far more dire.

The tough Midwesterner in me would love to say that I didn't shed a tear at that realization, but that would be a lie. My cheeks were damp more than once as I came to terms with what lay ahead. There were times when I wallowed in self-pity, wondering why this was happening to me. Other times, I stared out the window and wondered what the rest of my life would be like. Even after the first hearing aids, which *pumped up the volume*, I still struggled with bouts of despair. "Depression" is too strong a word, one that diminishes the struggle of millions who battle the disease. But I felt down and out with nowhere to turn.

Thankfully, a hero entered the picture.

I didn't know Nora all that well in college, but I knew of her. Indiana University, which is known by all who went there as IU, with its thirty thousand undergraduate students, was less like a major university and more like Hickory, the fictional town in the movie *Hoosiers*. Even if you didn't know everyone by name, you had heard of people; you knew their majors, or their hometowns, or the bars they frequented. I knew of Nora because of her name. You couldn't throw a basketball through a hallway in the Midwest without it bouncing off a couple of Jennys, Megans, or Laurens, but the only Noras I knew were grandmothers or nuns.

I first saw Nora in room 17 of the Phi Gamma Delta fraternity house as she studied for an organic chemistry exam with my roommate. Until that moment, I'd never understood what having your breath taken away meant. I'd played enough contact sports to understand having the wind knocked out of you, but this was different. I thought the whole "breathtaking" thing was hyperbole. You didn't lay eyes on someone for the first time and have trouble inhaling, or so I thought before having it happen. Not only did I feel my lungs catch when I saw Nora, it dawned on me that she was helping my smartest friends with their homework. It would take a while for me to realize just how brilliant she was, but I immediately got the sense that she was confident, engaging, and wholesome, in addition to being stunning. Nora was friendly in a way that wasn't at all flirty. She wasn't at the house "studying" as a pretext for anything else. She was doing schoolwork, and helping others, which turned out to be a microcosm of her character and personality.

With limited knowledge of hydrocarbons, I wasn't sure what to say to extend our interaction that first day. I just wondered how I'd spent four years in Bloomington without meeting her.

The weekend we both graduated from college, Nora and I ended up on a pontoon boat together. It was a lake party and our first chance to interact. The music was thumping, the sun was hot, and the beer was cold. Perfect, except she brought a date who looked like he'd just finished an Abercrombie photo shoot. It would have been awkward to spend much time with her, but there is only so much room on a pontoon boat.

Nora's smile was bigger and her laugh a little louder than everyone else's. I didn't catch much of the conversations she was having, but that didn't stop me from being drawn to her, even though I knew the chances of interacting in any meaningful way were slim. The easy, casual smile; the way she tilted her head back, so the sun hit her face at just the right angle; the way she seemed to engage every person on the boat in a way that felt special. I couldn't be the only one who noticed, could I?

Reality hit me fast. A relationship at that point was absurd. We were both graduating. That was the reason for the boat party. We were all passing through the same door into a hallway with dozens of different doors ahead, each of us nodding at our collective journey before saying our goodbyes.

I was graduating with a degree in marketing, with plans to be a brand manager. I wasn't entirely sure what that entailed, but I was drawn to the idea of being a part of the way the public views a person, product, or company, another instinct embedded into my subconscious as someone with a condition that affected my every interaction. I felt that developing strategies around brand building was a natural path for me. As I interviewed for those coveted entry-level positions with companies like Procter & Gamble, I met with the hiring managers for a company that sold ad space to those brand managers. As part of the recruiting process, I was invited to visit their offices in Chicago. Everything about the experience felt like the right fit for me.

Two things stood out. The hotel room where they housed me had a beautiful view of Lake Michigan and a wall-mounted phone by the toilet, which was something I'd never seen before. Also, the senior sales manager had a poster for the movie *Animal House* on the wall. If the company offered those kinds of wonders, this was where I was meant to be.

Riding the high of that recruitment, I ignored the advice

of pretty much everyone and countered their initial offer. Much to the shock and amazement of all my friends and family, they agreed. I felt flush with cash. The bonus alone represented six months of doing dishes at the fraternity house, which had been my job for the last three years. I had dreams of all the great stuff I'd get for my first apartment when that bonus check came. However, then came a crash course in income taxes. I found myself with just enough extra money to buy a new mattress.

Still, I felt more alive than ever. Lincoln Park, just north of the city, had everything a young Hoosier could want, and a lot more than I thought I would ever find given my hearing condition. I had navigated the waters of NF2 all the way to a college degree and a first job. The hearing aids I now wore—stopgap devices that wouldn't take away the tumors or arrest the inevitable fate that hung over me like the sword of Damocles—didn't detract from my ability to fit in socially or professionally, at least not yet.

My stages of grief had passed, and I'd accepted my condition and the future it promised (although there was still the occasional pang of fear), but romance seemed like a sunken treasure. What woman would want a lasting relationship with a guy who would inevitably lose all his hearing in the best-case outcome? My stages of grief might have passed, but the reality of my situation remained the same. As much as I tried to wave away my condition when I was with others, times like this made me feel like damaged goods.

I tried to push that familiar pang aside. For the moment, I hoped to enjoy a celebration with friends old and new, including the lovely Nora, who was on her way to Indianapolis to medical school. I hoped that our paths would cross again some-day soon, preferably without Abercrombie guy hovering around.

Before any of us knew it, six months passed, a blink of an eye for most, but an eternity for a group of young adults advancing through the postgrad stages of life. That same group of friends who had been together on the pontoon boat decided to throw a reunion party to celebrate our first half year as real-world adults. It was in Chicago on New Year's Eve that we would ring out the millennium and usher in the 2000s at a place called McGee's, a dive bar with one-dollar longneck beers and a menu item entitled "Big Ass Salad."

The bar was packed with people for whom the menu was perfect, and Prince's "1999" blared over the speakers. *"Two thousand zero, zero, party's over, oops, out of time."* I loved the *Purple Rain* era and would miss hearing Prince when the day came that I heard nothing at all, but just then the sound faded, not because of my hearing, but because of the pounding in my chest at who I saw across the room. Nora stood at the bar, drink in hand, chatting with a mutual friend. In a trick of the brain, a spotlight seemed to shine over her. Everyone else became shadows, even the date I had brought with me that night. It was the second time I'd been in Nora's company for a social gathering, and the second time decorum interfered.

I saw Nora dancing with herself, self-assured and fun-loving. As I stood at the bar, my date at my side, I pondered the least awkward way to ditch someone at 9:00 P.M. on New Year's Eve who was counting on me to drive her home.

When my date, a smart and dynamic young woman who deserved better than the halfhearted attempt I made at small talk, darted to the restroom, I sauntered over to say hello to Nora in the hopes that she would remember my name. To my relief, she did, and we chatted for a few minutes about her first semester of medical school and my foray into the workforce at News America Marketing. We chatted a moment longer. With my hearing aids and her medical knowledge, she expected me to look at her. I didn't have to explain my reliance on lipreading, especially in a loud bar. What she didn't know was that I couldn't look away. At that point in my life, I'd never uttered the word "smitten." It was from another time, like couples "courting" in a "parlor." Of course, I thought the name "Nora" fit perfectly in that time, so to say that I was smitten with her didn't seem out of place.

We drifted away and blended back into the celebration. As midnight approached, I turned to my poor neglected date and suggested that I get some champagne to ring in the New Year. The countdown was close. Prince came back, sizzling through the speakers—"*I was dreamin' when I wrote this / Forgive me if it goes astray.*" I timed my steps just right, maneuvering through the crowd and saying hello to people as casually as possible. "Eight . . . seven . . . six . . ." I got to the bar. I could have cut in front of the couple heading by me, but I needed another second and a half. "Four . . . three . . . two . . ." And there she was. I had finagled myself right next to Nora just as the countdown hit "One," and shouts of "Happy New Year!" went up everywhere. There were horns and fireworks. I feigned surprise at being by her in this moment. We smiled, and in that instant, shared our first kiss.

It seemed innocent enough, even though I had gone out of

my way to orchestrate the moment. But it also seemed natural, as if we were meant to be together. That was my take, at least. The funny thing is, more than two decades later, Nora has no recollection of that moment. All the trouble I went through to put myself in the right spot at the right time, and she doesn't remember it at all. In a way, that's perfect, because it reinforces how connected we were from the beginning. Why would she remember the first kiss when there were millions more to come?

I remember the moment, the kiss, like it was yesterday. The two of us drifted our separate ways again, and I took my date her glass of champagne.

The Backstreet Boys' *Millennium* album cheesed through the speakers, *"You are my fire / The one desire."*

On our first official date, Nora asked to see my latest MRI scans. I should have known we were meant for each other, but at the time, I couldn't think through my racing heart. The fact that we were in a long-distance relationship from the start should have made things more difficult, but instead, it kept me disciplined and appreciative. If she had been right next door, I might have taken her presence and all that went with it for granted. Because she was three hours away, toiling through the rigors of med school, a discipline I could only dream about but one that made me admire her as much as I adored her, I took every second as a gift.

Email became our magic medium, which worked out great for me. The keyboard levels the field for the hearing impaired. We would send each other notes about everything, the latest television shows we watched, or what she had learned in anatomy class. Many times, I would hold off opening her emails just to let the anticipation build. Everything she wrote excited me, even when it was routine. Her cadaver's name was Virginia Slim, for example. That was dark, but funny. Reading and rereading her notes let me get to know Nora through the formality of the written word, even when she was letting her guard down.

After a few weeks, we decided it was time to schedule regular visits. Depending on our schedules, she would make the drive north from Indy or I would drive south down I-65. Leaving Chicago at 5:00 P.M. was never a good idea, but I would plow ahead anyway, hoping for the best. I would even take the Skyway, with its $8.50 toll, to shave off a few minutes. Nora was worth it. Plus, Phish had recently released a six-CD live collection called *Hampton Comes Alive,* with forty-four songs. My favorite was a fifteen-minute-nine-second version of "Divided Sky," although they also recorded a cover of Will Smith's "Gettin' Jiggy wit It" that caused me to cringe. Even with hearing loss, some sounds rub you the wrong way. I channeled my excitement by rolling the windows of the Dodge Intrepid down and cranking the speakers up, playing "Divided Sky" on repeat, a dozen times in a row, for the entirety of the trip. It wasn't the lyrics that inspired me; there were very few. It was the crescendos connected with my internal drive to see her, long and hopeful.

Because everything about the early days of our relationship seemed like a throwback to another time, I would often wear my best suits for the trip, like a gentleman suitor taking a carriage to visit the mistress of the manor. Her next trip up, she'd meet me at work wearing a blue-sequined gown, which made her quite a sight at Penny's Noodle Shop, our standard spot for sharing a plate of pad thai.

Our weekends were scenes out of a movie: staying out late, sleeping in, strolling the sidewalks with nowhere to go. From the outset, we were open books. No games, no pretense: we were young adults who were transparent with each other and happy being together doing nothing at all. We'd go to Chicago's great parks and listen to Phish. I was far from a Deadhead, but I could belt out my fair share of Jerry Garcia greatest hits lyrics—"*Trouble ahead, trouble behind / And you know that notion just crossed my mind.*" Phish was our generation's answer to that genre. "*I took a moment from my day / Wrapped it up in things you say / And mailed it off to you.*"

Everything about Nora felt right. Contentment almost seemed too easy. Happiness was supposed to be harder than this, or so I'd always thought. You weren't supposed to find the right person and have everything fall into place. Life was supposed to be about challenges and striving for things. Having a person like Nora arrive so early and so easily seemed almost too good to be true. Our time together made me forget the inevitable. Only when she left, and I was alone in bed with my thoughts, did I slip into "what if" mode. What if my tumors grew quickly and I needed surgery right away? What would that do to our relationship? What if my hearing went completely south right away? How would that affect us? It was easy for someone to say, "I understand and will stand with you," in the abstract. The reality of a hospital room and a boyfriend who could no longer hear you was something else entirely. When she was with me, those thoughts were miles away. Alone at night, staring at the darkness, I felt as though I couldn't shake them from my brain. I knew I would have been lucky to have Nora as a friend. To be in a relationship with her was something I had never dreamed possible.

After our weekends, we'd go back to our email exchanges. Monday emails were my favorite. We got into the habit of re-counting the best and worst things that happened when we were together, which was like reminiscing through the written word. Those highlights included things like standing on a hay bale at the Guinness Oysterfest listening to the band Guster for the very first time. There was a picnic dinner, a shared foot-long sandwich from Subway, and a bottle of the most afford-able red blend, on the deck of a sailboat called *Wendy*, a cruise that included a fireworks show over Lake Michigan. One visit we tried sea urchin for the first and last time, and other times we'd take in a show.

Summer arrived and school let out. Nora spent more time in Chicago. Our neighborhood bartender learned her name, and we listened to Elvis on the jukebox—*"I'm caught in a trap / I can't get out / Because I love you too much, baby."*

Back home, we'd run through the playlists: Aerosmith—*"Talkin' 'bout things and nobody cares"*—and the Beach Boys. *"I love the colorful clothes she wears / And the way the sunlight plays upon her hair / I hear the sound of a gentle word / On the wind that lifts her perfume through the air."*

I introduced her to the haunting baritone of Johnny Cash—*"You've got a way to keep me on your side / You give me cause for love that I can't hide."*

At this point, my in-the-canal hearing aid had been doing

most of the heavy lifting. It worked so well that I thought sometimes that my diagnosis must have been incorrect. Or maybe I would be the one exception, the "medical miracle" that would end up in journals throughout the land. That fantasy often kept me from thinking about how each of the musical firsts I was sharing with Nora might also be a last.

In her first year, Nora had done research and cowritten a paper that was picked up by a major medical journal. So, as if she weren't already lapping me at every turn, she was now published. As part of that prestigious accomplishment, she traveled to New Orleans for a radiology event to be recognized and to get her noticed in all the right circles. When she returned, she shrugged the event off as if it was nothing, even though we both knew what an enormous honor it was be listed as one of the authors of a paper like that. Typical of her style, though, Nora fell right back into life.

She helped me move into a nicer apartment. As we carried boxes and chairs into the still-small place, I was wearing a T-shirt from an NF fundraiser that I'd attended, and she was in sweatpants. Beck was on the stereo, performing "Beautiful Way" just for us. *"Searchlights on the skyline / Just looking for a friend / Who's going to love my baby / When she's gone around the bend."*

That is when I began to think about the soundtrack. These were the moments I wanted branded on my brain. The flutters in my stomach, and the rushing of my heart as I took the dust rag out of Nora's hand, put her arm over my shoulder, and slow-danced in the living room: I wanted those lyrics of my life permanently imprinted in my memory.

"I think I'm falling in love with you," I told her.

We danced a few more beats until my roommate, still moving furniture, yelled from the back, "What the hell do box springs even do?"

Nora and I bent over in laughter.

A few weeks later, my neck began to hurt.

Hm, I thought, that's weird.

FOUR

I N SICKNESS AND IN HEALTH" IS A WEIGHTY PHRASE THAT YOU NEVER WANT TO THROW AROUND LIGHTLY. If you read it slowly and think about the words, there are no qualifiers. Nobody ever says, "Well, unless she gets really sick," or "Yeah, I'll buy him Tylenol and schedule the doctor's appointment, but there are limits." Even though everyone hears those words and can recite the phrases from memory—*for better and for worse; for richer and for poorer; in sickness and in health*—the reality is a lot heavier than the recitation, but because we've heard it so many times, we don't think through what it actually means.

Marriage, in the best of circumstances, presents all sorts

of challenges—financial, emotional, relational—and that's when everyone involved feels great, so it's certainly more difficult when one of you gets sick. Of course, when you are young, you often choose not to think about it. Two healthy people in love: What could possibly go wrong?

Unfortunately, life will go sideways on you at some point. It's not a question of if; it's when and how bad it will be. But in those tragic times, when bad news falls over you like a dark cloud, there are glimpses of beauty, inflections of love that penetrate beyond the ordinary. There is, in hardship, a depth and richness inside a relationship that you might never have otherwise found.

I was fortunate. From the moment I met Nora, we both knew my challenges. I also believed early in our relationship that I had found someone in this beautiful woman who understood that the words you recite at a wedding are not a list of things you promise to start on that day. Vows are an affirmation, a verbal punctuation on a commitment you made long before the day you walked down the aisle.

That is a life lesson that most young people—especially young men—don't learn often or early enough. I was blessed on that front. My tutor arrived in the form of a sharp, annoying pain that I couldn't identify.

Most people would have let it go, especially at my age. You're in your twenties, reasonably active with a healthy social life, and one day your neck starts hurting. The list of dismissive diagnoses you give yourself is as long as it is stupid, starting with "I slept on it wrong," and moving up to "I must have pulled a muscle." Ever since I was a kid, old men had talked about "getting a crick" in their necks. None of them bothered giving a symptomatic range or a proper medical definition for cricks, so I wasn't sure if this qualified. All I knew was that there was a pain around C2 and C3 that ranged from annoying to near debilitating. Sharp, dull, aching: the description varied but the pain never went away. I paid good money for massage therapy in the hope that this was a series of muscle spasms, something that warm heat and pressure would release. When that didn't work, I tried the bathtub. As soothing as that sounds, I lived with a couple of former fraternity brothers at the time, so the tub wasn't the most sanitary place in the apartment. Still, the angle of the porcelain and the temperature of the water—so hot I could barely put a toe in for a minute or two—seemed like a good idea. But far from easing my suffering, every remedy I attempted agitated the pain. It was like I had a clawing little gremlin holding a corkscrew at the base of my skull. Every time I swatted at him, he got angry and twisted the screw a little deeper into my neck.

I sought relief in a bottle—not alcohol, but prescription medications, which I got from my doctor. That slowed the gremlin, but at a cost that was almost as bad as the pain. The combination of Vicodin and steroids left me angry, hungry, swollen, and unable to sleep. I developed acne for the first time since junior high, and my face took on the shape and consistency of the moon. I had dry mouth and would sweat as if I'd just finished a workout. I knew there was a problem when I ate a large stuffed-crust pizza, in part because I never ate that much alone, but mostly because I wasn't hungry when I started and wasn't full when I finished. When I wasn't carb loading, I was snapping at anyone who suggested that I lay off the tubs of ice cream. The pain meds dulled more than the stabs in my neck. They left me with a constant hangover, the kind of brain fog that slows cognition and makes every movement feel like a chore. I was miserable and a wretch to be around. I'm certain that my roommates thought about bolting. If our signatures hadn't been on the lease together, I feel certain they would have said, "Matt, we love you, man, but we're going to have to find another place."

The one person who remained rock steady throughout was Nora, who took the brunt of my roid rage without a flinch. It helped that she was a med student who understood the side effects of the drugs I'd been prescribed. Still, nobody enjoys being snapped at by a juiced-up account coordinator in a cheap suit. Throw in the fact that she was still a long-distance girlfriend who could have her pick of future surgeons, cardiologists, endocrinologists, or any other ologist she wanted, and I am amazed that she stuck around with me through my chronic mood swings.

Not only did she not leave, but Nora became my advocate, taking a clinical approach to my pain. She read every study she could find on NF2 and spoke to numerous doctors about what I was experiencing. In the backs of our minds, we both had a sense that this was related to my condition, but this was also a path neither of us had ever walked. Thankfully, we were able to hold hands and take each step together.

This went on for the entire month of July, a time when

Nora was in Chicago and should have been enjoying strolls along the shores of Lake Michigan, visiting museums, and hanging out in all those great parks. Instead, she was busy confirming my MRI appointment and helping balance my pain mitigation.

I hate saying we both felt relieved when MRI day came, but I didn't like the person I had become. I knew Nora needed a break, even if it was just a day of me lying in the metal tube with the jackhammers pounding. Full head, neck, and spine MRIs take hours. You have to lie perfectly still, or the imaging won't work. It's like olden times when photographers had to get under a cloth hood while holding a flashbulb the size of a dinner plate. I thought about those cowboys and Civil War soldiers standing rigid for their photographs, all while the MRI machine banged and clanged up and down my body, taking advanced three-dimensional imagery of my anatomy. This is done by detecting the rotational axis of the protons in the water of living tissue, something my girlfriend understood and could explain to everyone except me, the marketing guy.

Motionless and cranky, I had time in that tube to think. When the day came that I lost my hearing—a time I had continued to shove into a dark corner until a hospital visit like this one reminded me that the steamroller was still coming, getting a little bigger each time I looked—when that day finally arrived, I vowed that I would not sound deaf. Maybe some of it was the steroids, and some my twenty-something-year-old ego, but the idea of being the guy who had trouble with vocal modulation, the person who lost opening and closing consonants like a faded childhood memory, that was something I promised myself would never happen. I had always been a verbal communicator, charming my teachers, selling my classmates, and persuading my bosses through the power of the spoken word. There is nothing like the art of a well-timed joke or a perfect line delivered for maximum impact. If someone says, "Hasta la vista, baby," your mind instantly hears it in an Austrian accent, because Arnold Schwarzenegger made it a cultural tagline. My career was marketing. It would be hard to build brands if I couldn't deliver messaging to clients. I didn't know a lot about my future at that point, but one goal I set for myself early was that I wanted to sound like me, even if I couldn't hear my own voice. I would practice my diction, take elocution lessons if necessary, but I would always speak with my voice.

I also didn't want to be viewed as different because I was deaf. I never wanted to see the involuntary flash of pity in someone's eyes, didn't want "special" dispensations, didn't want to be the object of anyone's virtue signals. The Matt who had been successful up to that point would be the same guy going forward, even after I could no longer hear anyone say, "Nice to meet you."

In marketing, the old adage is you can be good, you can be fast, and you can be cheap, but you can only pick two. I had three goals for my performance as a human. They were personal happiness, awareness of my time, and the quality of my contribution to the world. But I had no interest in picking just two.

The MRI machine continued to bang away. Every now and then a voice would come through one of the speakers. "How you doing in there, Matt?"

I would love to scratch my nose, rub my eyes, fluff up this pillow, and roll over onto my side, but other than that, everything's peachy. Instead of saying that, I shot them a silent thumbs-up.

I tried to block out the rattle by playing music in my head. *"Lady Madonna / Children at your feet / Wonder how you manage / To make ends meet."*

What was the next line? I struggled for a second to get it. *"Who finds the money / When you pay the rent . . ."*

I didn't want to lose those memories, either. I had played the Beatles in my bedroom when I was a kid. The way Paul changes keys twice in "I've Got a Feeling," or the barely contained emotion in George's voice as his *"guitar gently weeps,"* those were things I could not imagine losing. They brought back the feel of the thin carpet in my parents' basement, where the "good" Onkyo stereo lived against the wall, or the way the speakers on my Dodge Aspen conked out at even a hint of bass. They reminded me of mowing our one-acre yard on a dated riding mower with my Sony Discman and upgraded headphones. So many of those details were tied to the music of my childhood. I couldn't forget them.

There were many others, too. Long before rap was a thing, there was the spoken-word ballad of "A Boy Named Sue," the rhythm of which rang through my ears as the clatter of the magnets inside this coffin-sized contraption kept the perfect Johnny Cash beat.

Bam, Bam, Clack, Clack, Bam . . . *"I busted a chair right across his teeth / And we crashed through the wall and into the street / kickin' and a-gougin' in the mud and the blood and the beer."*

That was my dad's music. Forgetting it would be like forgetting him. Lying there in that sterile room with that pristine machine measuring the speed of my protons, praying that nature didn't call and force us to start over, I began to list the songs that I wanted to commit to memory forever, the ones that I would want to hum and sing in the right key long after I could no longer hear them. Who would be on the list? The Beach Boys were obvious, darn near every track on *Pet Sounds*. *"God only knows what I'd be without you."*

That was how I felt about Nora in that moment. She continued to stick with me, even though my immediate health and long-term prognosis remained unknown, although the best-case scenarios weren't great. My own family would have understood if Nora had backed away.

Instead, she navigated the waters of a burgeoning relationship with a guy who had a rare medical condition that would one day rob him of his hearing, a man who lived in another state and was in an entirely different field of work. And she did all this while excelling in medical school. God only knows, indeed.

There were so many songs that I needed to memorize. Simon and Garfunkel would make the list. Given my current situation, "The Boxer" seemed like one I would want to burn into my brain. *"In the clearing stands a boxer / And a fighter by his trade / And he carries the reminders / of every glove that laid him down."* I had a greater appreciation for that song because in the end, *"the fighter still remains."*

Let's hope.

I would need to memorize some Prince songs, although I couldn't imagine how I would sound singing "Purple Rain," even when my hearing was good. There would be some from my fellow Hoosier John Mellencamp. *"I've been doing it since I was a young kid and I come out grinnin' / Well, I fight authority, authority always wins."*

"Okay, Matt, that should do it," the voice said, snapping me back to the present and the test.

"Great," I said in a voice I hoped didn't sound sarcastic.

"You did well. Wait outside and someone will let you know when the results are ready."

As complex as this imagery was, I didn't expect it to be Polaroid quick. But the longer Nora and I waited, the more anxious we became. It wasn't as if we were waiting on Skippy from InstaPrint to give us eight-by-ten glossies of our stroll around Lincoln Park. This could be the day, the moment of truth. Maybe it was good news. Maybe the doctors were gathering around the screen wondering where my NF2 tumors had gone and what medical journals they should contact to publish their findings. Somewhere in the back of my mind, I heard Jefferson Starship. *"If only you believe in miracles, baby / So would I."*

We had lunch at the McDonald's connected to Riley Hospital, which turned out to be an underappreciated benefit of being grandfathered into care at the Children's Hospital in Indianapolis, where I was first diagnosed. When we returned to the basement MRI waiting room Nora heard, "The doctor's ready for you," from a smiling young technician. Nora stood quickly, and I felt a jolt of energy run through me like a shock. Was this what it felt like when a jury handed over a verdict and the judge said, "The defendant will rise"?

Five minutes later, Nora and I were standing close. I brushed my chest against her shoulder blade and nudged and felt a strand of her hair tickle the side of my neck. Together we stared at the shadowy gray image on a screen. For all the technology involved in MRIs, the images still looked grainy and vague to someone like me. Still, with a little prompting, I recognized the image of my spinal cord near the base of my brain. The three-inch milky-white highlight down the middle of the film, we were told, was a tumor and the spinal fluid it was clogging.

Any sort of "clog" is a bad thing. When your kitchen drain clogs, you have a problem. Toilet clogs are worse. Clogged arteries can lead to heart attacks or strokes. But as it turns out, spinal clogs are the worst. The doctor continued to go through his lecture on what we were seeing, while Nora nodded and asked medical-sounding questions. I didn't say much, because I knew that the day had finally come. My auditory-nerve tumors had taken a big, stretching yawn before branching out to see what else they could destroy. The target they picked was my spine.

"We'll need to schedule you for surgery," the doctor said.

I ran through my checklist of things going on at work. There were a couple of projects I could clear up in about two weeks, and one big account I would need to transition to a colleague. I told the doctor that we should be able schedule him just after Labor Day.

I can't remember if he chuckled out loud, but the sentiment was there.

"We're doing this day after tomorrow," he said. "Be here at six in the morning."

FIVE

I JUST WANT TO LIVE WHILE I'M ALIVE

IT'S MY LIFE

—Bon Jovi

THERE'S A GREAT BOOK WRITTEN MORE THAN HALF A CEN-TURY AGO BY AN AUSTRIAN NEUROLOGIST AND PSYCHIATRIST NAMED VIKTOR FRANKL. It's called *Man's Search for Meaning*, and it was first published in 1946. I read it because it was mentioned frequently by people in one of those Twitter threads about great books. Those people who praised it were right. Once I opened it, I couldn't put it down. Frankl recounts his time in the Theresienstadt concentration camp, where his father died of starvation, and Auschwitz, where his mother and sister were gassed. Frankl, while fighting to survive himself, noticed something significant about his fellow captives. Those who had no mission in life, nothing left to accomplish, died quickly, while those who kept specific goals in mind lived longer, many surviving until liberation. Sometimes the prisoners' goals were noble, things like getting back to family or rebuilding a business, for example. For others it was revenge against the Nazi guards. The morality of the goal didn't seem to matter. Whatever it was, having a specific mission seemed to help keep people alive. Frankl named his philosophy logotherapy, a stark departure from the Freudian theories of the day. Today, Frankl's thinking is so mainstream that it gets taken for granted. Almost everyone knows someone who defied expectations and outlived a terminal prognosis because they wanted to see their grandchildren graduate, or they needed to outlive their spouse. Some people are so driven by their work that they defy the odds of terrible diseases just to get a product to market or complete a project. Others, especially in our most recent wars, lost limbs and sustained incredible trauma, but battled back to their families because of promises they had made to return home.

Frankl's theories are now axioms of everyday existence. Goals give life meaning. They force you to refocus your mind when things go sideways.

My surgery didn't go as I had hoped. Like most people who go under the knife, I didn't know much about what happened in there. I met the anesthesiologist, who told me to count backward from ten, and I didn't get to eight before the lights went out. When I came out of it, I felt like no time had passed. I got to skip the anxious hours in the waiting room, thumbing through ancient magazines and trying to make small talk. But all that anxiety and more flooded my system when I woke up.

I couldn't feel my legs. I could see them. They were still there. My feet splayed out under the sheet, but I couldn't feel anything. I tried to pull my knees up. They worked, but not well. Then I tried to flex my ankles. I could move, but it was as if I were operating an avatar. I couldn't feel a thing. It was like having your hand fall asleep, really asleep, to the point where it doesn't even tingle but is just a blank spot where your hand used to be. Even if your fingers move, you can't feel it. That was the sensation I had over half my body. What began as a weird curiosity rapidly devolved into panic. Why couldn't I feel my legs? And when would I get some ice chips for the fire smoldering in my throat?

Nora came in and smiled. That calmed me down a little but didn't answer the most critical questions. What had happened, and when would I regain feeling? Then she said words that jolted me in ways I couldn't have imagined a few hours before: "We think you'll be able to walk again."

It turns out that removing a tumor from your spinal cord isn't like cutting a diamond. It's more like digging the last Pringle out of a can: messy, imprecise, and uncertain. Even if you get what you're after, you're likely to break some stuff along the way.

There are eight cervical pairs of nerves in the spinal cord, but there are one hundred billion neurons and more fibers than anyone can count. As advanced as modern medical equipment can be, when you're trying to cut out a tumor, you have to move a few things around. In my case, the surgeons had to shift some tissue and fibers out of the way and leave them there for half the day. Once the tumor was removed, the nerves and muscles snapped back into the right spots. But it's like the waistband in your favorite old pair of pants: once you stretch it and hold it for a while, it never goes back exactly as it was. When you're talking about jeans or sweatpants, a stretched waistband is an annoyance. When you're talking about nerves, you wake up from anesthesia and see your toes as alien objects. Then, when the best thing your girlfriend can say is "We think you'll be able to walk again," you're left wondering if any of this was a good idea.

I was reminded of that truck ride to the Army physical with my dad a few years earlier. Dylan warned me something was coming, *"For the times, they are a-changin'."*

Hard tasks are a prerequisite for human advancement, an opportunity for growth and, eventually, a way to make life better for those who come next. A lot of children shivered in the cold before some medieval engineer invented the internal fireplace and stone chimney. A lot of what we take for granted today is the result of a hardship. People struggle with a particular thing until someone creates a solution.

I wasn't lying in my hospital bed contemplating a cure for lower-body nerve damage. My overwhelming feeling at the time was panic. While I had rarely had trouble playing the tough hands I was dealt, that was mostly because I didn't have much choice. I took each challenge as it came. Solve one puzzle, fix one problem, and then move on to the next. Remembering the emotional toil of those episodes is another matter. I can recall all the factual details of what I endured. There's no trouble reciting the details of diagnoses, surgeries, side effects, and recoveries. My trouble has always been wrapping my arms around the helplessness, coming to terms with the feeling of being less than complete. Marinating in the misery and ugliness of what I went through accomplishes nothing and would come off as whiny, which I never was. But as time has passed, my retelling of the events surrounding my NF2 experience has become watered down. I try to pepper every detail with a joke or a phrase like "getting better every day," which has always been a coping mechanism, a self-taught lesson in stoicism and a way of avoiding the fear I felt in those moments.

Thinking back on those days, I am reminded of Bill Belichick, the coach of the New England Patriots of the NFL. After one particular *Monday Night Football* loss, Belichick held his regular press conference and answered every single question with the same answer: "We are looking ahead to Cincinnati," which was the next game on the Patriots' schedule. I knew exactly what Coach Belichick meant. If you keep moving forward, focusing on what's ahead, you can avoid the devastation behind you. Since you can't change the past, I thought that dwelling on it, even in the form of processing my feelings, was unproductive, so I didn't do it. I marched ahead, focusing on the next problem to solve. Much later, I realized that even if I didn't acknowledge those feelings, I still had to deal with them eventually.

My surgeon finally checked in, and I asked a lot of pointed questions, but the answers were vague. You never want to hear

"We don't know" from doctors, especially when you can't feel anything from the waist down and nurses are stretching panty hose over your legs to protect against blood clots. Instead of outcomes, the doctors focused on process. By day three in the ICU, where I had grown right sick of listening to the guy next to me groan as he yanked at his catheters all day, I was irritable and impatient, one of the typical coping mechanisms that men use to mask fear. Still, a full seventy-two hours of doing nothing to get me walking again seemed preposterous. I had walked into that hospital expecting to walk out. No rehab or answers was *no bueno*.

"Nerves are not an exact science," the specialist told me. "They heal or not at their own pace. Where we are a year from now is where we will be."

We? There was no "we." I was the one who'd strolled in here on two good legs and was now being told that I might never walk again. And while I was no math whiz, the three days I'd been lying in the ICU feeling ignored constituted somewhere around 1 percent of the total time I felt my doctor had given me to relearn to walk.

That was when I went full Belichick and set my mind to the next goal. Despite the real possibility that I would be in a wheelchair for the rest of my life, I decided right then and there that I would, as soon as possible, run a marathon. I'd never done it. At that moment, I wasn't sure how far a marathon was. When I ran track in high school I was always at or near the bottom of every field I entered. I once finished third in a four-hundred-meter race, earning a custom-made ribbon with gold lettering that provided memorable context to my feat; in all caps it read THIRD. The fact that there were only three runners didn't bother me at all. I got major props for sticking with it, even though I was the slowest runner in southern Indiana. Even so, I always had goals. This was no different. Not only would I walk again, I would run. And not just a step or two. I would run the classic distance race since the age of the ancient Greeks, the span between the city of Marathon and the Acropolis in Athens. When the Greeks defeated the Persians in the battle of Marathon, a messenger named Pheidippides ran just over twenty-six miles to the highest point in the city, where he declared "Nike," which is the ancient Greek word for "victory." I played that romantic story over and over in my mind. That was my logotherapy, my "focusing on Cincinnati," my mission that would push me through this trauma.

My thinking was simple but clarifying. Marathons are hard. I don't want to get back to the bare minimum. I want to, once again, do the difficult things. My reality, though, was more along the lines of "Get comfortable in this wheelchair, because you might be in it for a long time."

Unable to move around on my own, I would need to relocate to a rehab facility. We failed to let some friends know that it was *physical* rehab, and, years later, they told me how proud they were of me for overcoming substance abuse.

Thanks to Nora's dogged research and some family connections, we were able to find a bed at a long-term care center, one geared for an older population, in Evansville, close to my parents' house. I heard Nora on the phone with my employer. We knew each other well enough at that point that I recognized her tone, a mixture of professional doggedness and anxious apprehension. "We don't know how long it will be," I heard her say, followed by a "Thank you so much. I will let him know." Then I sensed a change in her voice, a not-quite-tearful relief. "You're going to continue to pay him?" she said. "Oh, that's great. Thank you so much."

Rehab finally began with something less than a bang. My first day involved being introduced to the gym equipment. I didn't get to use it; I just got to meet it. That was bound to ready me for a 26.2-mile run in no time.

Nora moved in with my parents and brought me Subway sandwiches every day, a reprieve from the mashed potatoes and baked carrots at the facility's cafeteria. She would lie with me on the tiny single bed with its threadbare sheets and tell me about her own training. Nora had also decided to run a marathon, as a fundraiser for NF2 research. I wasn't sure at the time if she made the decision in solidarity with me, or because she doubted that I would ever be able to run a race on my own. Either way, I felt elated that she would be joining me. Nora's father had a minor muscular disorder that caused his muscles to lock briefly. It wasn't something most people noticed, but it made her family hyperaware of people who were battling challenges. She always said that she couldn't imagine health being a factor in a relationship. "A person in perfect condition could get hit by a bus tomorrow," she said.

She came to the rehab center every day, sometimes to deliver food and do a clinical analysis of my progress, other times to watch old movies and tell jokes. There was an old VCR built into the small television in my room, a high-tech feature in the eighties that seemed like something out of *The Flintstones* by the turn of the millennium. But that added to the charm, especially when I introduced Nora to cult classics like *This Is Spinal Tap* and *Strange Brew*. Something about the Mackenzie brothers from that era still brings a smile to my face. *"You hosers get me a fresh case of beer first thing in the morning."* Most people would consider it guy humor, but Nora let out some full-throated chortles at the right spots.

The fact that she seemed content doing little more than hanging out with her rehabbing boyfriend while eating Orville Redenbacher's microwave popcorn made me sense something that I'd never felt around anyone outside my family. It was like an internal warmth, a contentment that I didn't have to do anything to find. I wasn't chasing excitement with Nora. This wasn't the thrill of infatuation. I'd already been there. About the most exciting thing at rehab was to sneak outside with a wheelchair. Nora would push me around the grounds, our faces turned up to bathe in the sun. Then we'd sneak into Eastland Mall. Nora would put a ski cap on my head to hide the shaved area and the stitches, and we'd cruise the stores. This was happiness. This was love.

At that moment I knew that I would ask Nora to marry me. She was the one. Not to try to bill myself as a relationship counselor, but when a beautiful woman who is smart and driven enough to be in med school, fit enough to run a marathon, thoughtful enough to raise money for your rare neurological condition, and patient and confident enough to move in with your parents sticks with you while you relearn how to walk, you would be a fool not to marry her. Those are the rules.

I considered asking Nora to marry me right then and there, maybe over a meatball sub during the toga-party scene of *Animal House*. Then I realized that proposing would be tough. I couldn't get down on one knee, and our wheelchair escapes made it difficult to shop for a ring. But I knew. With the faint smell of urine and the bark of one of the meanest nurses I've ever met in the distance, I realized beyond any doubt that Nora was the one, the person I wanted to have by my side for the rest of my life, "for richer and for poorer; in sickness and in health."

Then, like almost all men at that moment of realization, I let doubt creep in, not second-guessing, but worry that there were two parties involved in this process and one of them had every right to say no. Nora was almost too perfect. I thought she would be headed back to med school the following semester and I would be wheeling myself from the dining room to the nurses' station. It wouldn't have been fair.

I found myself humming an old Chicago song. *"If you leave me now / You'll take away the biggest part of me."*

My leg movement improved, slower than I wanted but with steady progress. I've always thought patience was an overrated virtue, so I was less than subtle about what I considered a lack of legitimate therapy. Finally, a new therapist showed up and met me in the parking lot with traffic cones and a medicine ball. My job was to raise a leg onto the cone and catch the ball, then raise the other leg and throw it back. In the weeks that passed, I graduated from my wheelchair to become a very unstable member of the foldable-walker community. The tennis balls on the feet of the walker were like badges of honor. A few weeks later I was proudly moving about with a cane and all the grace of a hippo. I stumbled about slowly and with assistance, but I was upright and moving. Each step got me closer to my marathon, which I now thought of as our marathon. Nora and I would train together, soon, or so I imagined as I took each wobbly step with the kind of cane that I'd seen octogenarians use to walk down the aisles at church.

As "straight line" as that rehab sounds, it's the Saturday morning cartoon version of how I felt at the time, part of my coping mechanism that leaves out the parts I taught myself to forget, or never processed in the first place. There's an indescribable terror that comes with waking up paralyzed and not having a clear answer as to whether or not you will feel or move your legs ever again. There's an anger at the surgeons who put you in that wheelchair, even though you were the one unwilling to study the risks ahead of time. There's a hopelessness that adds labor to every movement. And there are tears. Men feel a need to be strong. Providing and protecting are built into our DNA, and no amount of evolution will wipe that out. Throughout my life, I had also been the kind of guy who did things. Always up for a road trip to Canada or a quick climb up the town water tower, from cliff diving to whitewater kayaking, I was up for any challenge, and, to my adult shame, I tended to look askance at those who didn't do things. Now, in a matter of a week, I had gone from being the guy everyone admired for overcoming obstacles and living well with a rare disease, to a grown man who could not get to the toilet without a call button and an assist from two strangers. Nora would leave the room during those private moments, but there is no depth to the levels of shame I felt. Here was this woman I would normally be trying to impress with a dry joke or a comforting hug, and instead she was waiting outside a mesh curtain while two other women wiped me.

With whom do you share those feelings? Do you pour out your angst to the smiling face standing by your hospital bed? What do you say to those people who just want to know you are okay? If, in those moments, I had confessed my fear, if I had cut open the swelling vein of feelings and let all my emotions spill out, my condition would have remained unchanged. I still wouldn't have been able to feel my legs, and the steamroller of deafness would have still been growing larger on the horizon. Sharing those feelings would have only added weight onto those who loved me. So, I smiled and channeled my terror into an obsession with getting better.

As the hall walking improved and I became more self-sufficient with my bathroom visits, I knew it was time to head back to Chicago, which meant that Nora could move out of my parents' house. As I was packing my few belongings, Nora came to me and said, "We need to talk."

That's never good. In this case, Nora sat close to me and looked me in the eyes. I expected the worst. This was the part where she said, "I care about you, but I cannot be with you," or "It's not you, it's me," or the lamest of them all, "I love you, but I'm not in love with you." Instead, she told me that she had decided not to go back to med school.

My first instinct was sadness. I was sure Nora had made

this decision because of me. If that was the case, she would eventually regret it. When that day came, I would be the person she blamed. Nora had been by my side all summer and throughout my rehab. It seemed logical that she'd come to this decision because of my condition. When I pleaded with her not to drop out for me, she cocked her head, smiled, and said, "Why would you think this is about you?"

I had to chuckle at that one. Everything for the better part of two months had been about my recovery, so it wasn't too egotistical for me to assume she was doing this for me. Nora's independence was more attractive than her intelligence or physical beauty. And she is brilliant and gorgeous. In that moment, she assured me that she had been thinking about leaving med school for a while. She loved medicine and the idea of helping people, but the work-life balance of being a doctor did not align with how she wanted to live. If she was tops in her class, which no one doubted would be the case, she would have two more years of school before her residency, which often entailed working thirty-hour shifts in a hospital and being on call for another eighteen hours after that. Assuming everything went perfectly, she would be an internist or go into private practice at age thirty, after which she would spend countless hours wading through insurance regulations, billing procedures, and liability laws, all of which would cut back on the time she could spend with patients.

Hearing her explain it made me feel better. I could understand her reasoning, and I could see that this wasn't a decision she had made in haste. Nora thought things through. It was one of the things that would have made her a great doctor.

We made it back to Chicago after six weeks of full-time rehab. Nora's parents lived about thirty miles outside the city, so she lived with them, but she spent a lot of time in my garden apartment. My cane stride improved enough that I upgraded my four-prong "as seen on TV" version to the single leg, the Ferrari of canes. My life required finding small wins where I could, and single-legged canes were a dapper win. I went from hobbling like a guy who might fall with every step to limping with distinction. I could even tap the cane to the beat of whatever song I was singing as Nora and I walked the streets of the city. "*Wasn't me she was foolin' / 'Cause she knew what she was doin' / When she taught me how to walk this way.*" Steven Tyler gets me.

Nora got a job selling pharmaceuticals in a territory just south of Chicago. During the interview process, she was asked to describe her most difficult sell, and Nora told the story of explaining to her dad why she wasn't going back to medical school. That raised the eyebrows of the human resources officer and got a few smiles from the sales executives. They couldn't wait to hire her.

I went back to work at my marketing job, and continued the long, hard process of rehabilitation. Despite my best efforts to get back to full energy, I was in bed by eight every evening. The two of us settled into a routine. She would head into the city on Friday, we'd spend a few hours looking for precious street parking in Lincoln Park, and she'd stay until Monday morning. We'd hit Caribou Coffee, and she'd drop me off at my office and drive to the South Side to sell drugs.

Music became more important as the reality of hearing

loss intensified. Plus, with Nora and me both working, we had enough money to go to concerts, which we did in a flurry. At the United Center, the house Michael Jordan built, we had second-row seats for Paul McCartney. We stood through most of the show, and I sang at the top of my lungs for much of the night. *"Love was such an easy game to play / Now I need a place to hide away . . ."*

When Beck came to the Chicago Theatre, we got seats in the first row of the balcony and swayed to the beat. *"Whisperin' her love through a smoke ring smile / She doesn't know what happens when she's around / I think I'm in love / But it makes me kinda nervous to say so."*

We crossed over the state line into Wisconsin to go to the Alpine Valley Resort, where we camped out and watched Phish bounce around onstage, our version of driving a psychedelic VW bus to a Grateful Dead show. Then we headed back to our home state, where we sat on the lawn for the Dave Matthews Band at a place called Deer Creek in Indianapolis. *"I am no hero, oh, that's for sure / But I do know one thing / Is where you are is where I belong / I do know where you go is where I want to be."*

I'm not sure how we ended up with U2 tickets at Allstate Arena, near O'Hare Airport, but they were the worst seats in the building. That didn't stop either of us from raising our arms and letting go when Bono and the Edge ripped into "With or Without You." And I can't remember where we saw Jimmy Buffett, which is not unusual for many of the Parrot Heads who wasted away in Margaritaville. But that didn't stop this landlocked Hoosier from letting it rip. *"Son of a son of a sailor / Son of a gun / Load the last ton / One step ahead of the jailer."*

Concerts ranked just below rent and food on our monthly budgets. Whether or not we realized it at the time, we drank in each show with a sense of urgency. These weren't casual live-music experiences. We were imprinting memories onto our collective psyche, moments we could fall back on when the silence finally came. And we had Prince, Tom Petty, Bob Dylan, and a gang of their friends to help us prepare for that fateful moment.

I deliberately chose not to propose over Christmas. Nora's birthday was in February, and I wanted our engagement to stand alone as its own thing. So, on January 26, 2002, an unseasonably warm day in Bloomington surrounding no holiday at all, I snuck off to buy flowers. We were staying in the Century Suites that Friday night because I had scored tickets to an IU basketball game the following day (the Hoosiers beat a ranked Illinois team and set a Big Ten record for most three-pointers made in a game, a fact that only devoted fans of college hoops would ever remember). During dinner, I was so nervous that I didn't touch my drink. Then we headed over to the Rose Well House on the Indiana campus, a beautiful old meeting space with a limestone gazebo built in 1908. I had Nora cover her eyes as I put flowers and tea candles around the gazebo. Then I put Anne Murray on the battery-powered boom box that I'd brought. *"I'll always remember / The song they were playing / The first time we danced, and I knew."*

We slow-danced like high schoolers. Then I got down on one knee, no small feat given that I hadn't been able to walk five months before. When I proposed, Nora put her hand over her mouth and said, "Oh, my gosh. Oh, my gosh." I wasn't sure if that was a yes, but I got the sense that she had accepted. We stopped at a grocery store on the way back to the hotel, and Nora bought a bridal magazine to start making plans.

Six months after that, within a year of my surgery, I finished my first marathon, with Nora by my side. Technically, she was slightly ahead of me, but I felt like I'd earned the right to call it a draw. Bon Jovi and Frankel knew it all along. *"I ain't gonna live forever / I just want to live while I'm alive."*

Mission accomplished.

The question I didn't ask out loud at the time, but the one that kept knocking at the back of my brain, was: Okay, now what?

SIX

I N THE OPENING BARS OF LYNYRD SKYNYRD'S "SWEET HOME ALABAMA," THE FIRST WORDS THE LEAD SINGER, RONNIE VAN ZANT, SAYS ARE "TURN IT UP." For decades, I thought he was speaking to me and all the other listeners, imploring us from the grave (Van Zant was killed in the famous plane crash in 1977) to crank up the volume and get our groove on to this southern rock classic. Turns out he was talking to Rodney Mills, the sound engineer in the control room of Studio One in Doraville, Georgia, where the band recorded their first three albums. Van Zant couldn't hear Ed King's guitar intro.

The singer needed the volume in his headphones turned up. Al Kooper, who produced Skynyrd for MCA Records, left Van Zant's line in the final cut so that, three generations later, people would hear "Turn it up" and do just that.

I thought about that line a good bit in the early 2000s, not because I was a rabid Skynyrd fan, but because I felt like every note in the song of my life was being turned down. I no longer heard music in stereo. Surround sound meant nothing. In the course of a few short years my hearing had gone from impaired to almost not there; from four big speakers with a subwoofer to a transistor radio on the other side of the room. The thing about gradual hearing loss is that you forget when you used to hear something that you no longer can. Just as, in many cases, we don't know what we don't know, we don't hear the things we don't hear. That's the opposite of sight. If you don't see a road sign clearly, you don't blame the Department of Transportation worker for using a blurry font. You know right away that it's time to see the optometrist. When I reached the point where I couldn't read a sign, that was on me. I knew my eyes were going bad. But even after I knew I was losing my hearing and would one day be completely deaf, I still turned up the stereo volume, assuming that the speakers were bad, and still asked people to repeat themselves, assuming that they mumbled. That must have been another defense mechanism.

After my surgery, I began to listen to my soundtrack with some intention. That was the time when I put the songs on repeat and focused on each note, doing everything I could to get the beats just right.

These were the early days of internet search engines, and song lyrics were just being made available online. I would print out lyrics if I didn't have liner notes from the album or CD, which is how everyone listened to music back when streaming was what tin miners did to ore. Sometimes I had to go to Sam Goody or Tower Records, long-lost relics of an ancient civilization, to buy an album just so I could replay the songs and get the lyrics right.

In that process, I realized I had misheard a lot of stuff over the years. Toto wasn't speculating about weather conditions by singing "I guess it rains down in Africa." Elton wasn't saying, "I can't lie, no more of you darlin'." It was *"I can't light no more of your darkness."* Wow, that made a lot more sense. And the Rocket Man was not "burring up the fumes and pheromones." He was *"burning up the fuse up here alone."* It seemed simple and a little embarrassing once you read it.

As I assembled my life playlist, I spent time thinking about what each song meant and why it was worth remembering. Like the pencil marks on the doorframe to show how much you've grown, each song I found was a marker of how I was changing.

Despite the fact that his formative years coincided with the British Invasion, Dad's tastes leaned heavily to something best described as "anything with four brothers crooning." I was one of the only kids in our town to have an extensive collection of Statler Brothers records on hand just in case their grandparents needed a DJ.

Mom and Dad kept vinyl albums in a container near an old turntable he'd had since college. My generation now sees full-sized, two-sided albums, ten to twelve songs played on a boxy contraption with an arm and a needle, as authentic and cool. Dad's generation found them to be a chore. Nothing was more annoying than having to get up and turn an album over to side two. Then you had to clean the needle and hope the vinyl didn't get scratched. Our older siblings started with cassette tapes and then the digital magic of CDs. Thank goodness the millennial generation took it to the next level by inventing downloads—ten thousand songs on a device the size of a credit card in your pocket. Now, vinyl is back, outselling purchased downloads almost two to one. Seeing the delivery system for music come full circle has been a surprise for me. But at the time I was going through Mom and Dad's records, I was looking back, not ahead. It was evident Dad loved music that told stories.

The Return of Roger Miller was still in there. *"Trailer for sale or rent / rooms to let, fifty cents / No phone, no pool, no pets / I ain't got no cigarettes."*

I thumbed through the albums a little quicker until Johnny Cash jumped out, sweaty and hard, his eyes dark and unflinching. *Johnny Cash at Folsom Prison* had been another of the seminal albums of my childhood. Any connoisseur of classic country knows the tracks: "Folsom Prison Blues," "Orange Blossom Special," "Jackson." When I was a boy, the tougher, darker songs stayed with me. I didn't identify with them, but I was curious thinking that there were people who did. *"I hear the train a-comin' / It's rollin' 'round the bend / And I ain't seen the sunshine since I don't know when."*

Cash typified the men of my father's generation, sturdy

and upright, repentant for the sins that had hardened them. They were chiseled by the sharp edges of life. Men like Cash worked the fields in the bitter cold of a Midwestern winter. They were the men who could listen to an engine and know exactly what nut to tighten or what hose to replace; the men who went to school board and town hall meetings, not because they wanted to, but because it was their duty; the men who fed a nation before going home every night to say grace for a tableful of kids. Some of Cash's songs seemed hokey to my friends, especially those who were into Dr. Dre and Run-DMC, but they had never heard Johnny at his best. I can almost feel a small headache when I hear him sing his pal Kris Kristofferson's words, *"And the beer I had for breakfast wasn't bad / So I had one more for dessert."* Those lyrics would make the folks over at Death Row Records nod with approval. I had to imprint them into my mind for the memories they held.

From Dad's collection, I learned everything I know about shipping by listening to Gordon Lightfoot. *"That good ship and crew was a bone to be chewed / when the gales of November came early."*

The Irish Rovers' *Greatest Hits* taught me all about unicorns. And Ray Stevens's "The Streak" was the well-worn high-water mark of clever songwriting: *"Oh, yes, they call him the streak / Fastest thing on two feet."*

Then came the music of my teen years, which was a solid mix of oldies and radio hits. When my best friend turned sixteen, he bought a blue-and-white late-seventies pickup with an I-beam for a front bumper, the kind of thing that looked like a cowcatcher on the front of a train. We would climb aboard, turn on the aftermarket stereo he'd installed, and cruise through town to Axl Rose howling "Sweet Child o' Mine." Those were my macho days, when Bad Boy Matt would belt out the chorus of some Def Leppard tune—"Pour Some Sugar on Me"—while hanging my wrist over the passenger-side mirror and throwing my head back to acknowledge another kid with a cool nod. I considered AC/DC the edge of my hard-core rebellion. *"Knocking me out with those American thighs,"* indeed.

When that same friend sold the truck and bought a Jeep Wrangler with faux cowhide seats and a Diver Down flag on his front license plate, our tastes drifted back in time. Discovering the Eagles two decades late was a revelation. We weren't hard core. It was *Greatest Hits* stuff at best. But those songs also spoke to our need to carve our own ways. *"It may be rainin', but there's a rainbow above you / You better let somebody love you (let somebody love you) / You better let somebody love you, before it's too . . . late."*

The more I listened to and memorized the songs of Glenn Frey and Don Henley, the more I realized that they tickled more than a memory or two. Line after line churned up feelings from specific moments from my past, the smell of a spring dogwood blossom or the cool splash of a friend jumping off a dock and into the lake. *"Every time I try to walk away / something makes me turn around and stay / I can't tell you why / No, I can't tell you why."* Those were the moments I had to remember as I came to grips with the soundless world I was about to enter.

"Ain't it funny how your new life didn't change things? / You're still the same old [person] you used to be." I certainly hoped that

was the case. A deaf Matt would be more patient and more empathetic, but at what cost? I didn't know, and that scared me.

Because of the era in which I started to break away from
my parents, the music I listened to veered toward the stuff
they considered noise. Fat Boys, MC Hammer—"U Can't
Touch This"—DJ Jazzy Jeff and the Fresh Prince: that was the
music I turned up, which made it hard to find songs we could
all agree to listen to in the car. That was where Paul Simon
came in. The only cassette tape I ever wore out—and by that,
I mean I played it so much that the tape stretched, and the
sound became distorted—was *The Concert in Central Park*. Like
the Eagles' *Their Greatest Hits*, this was a compilation album
of Paul and Artie's best stuff, although in this case, it came
from a live performance. It started out as a compromise between my dad and me, and ended up being the kind of music
where, two bars in, we both found ourselves tapping our feet
and singing along.

I remember when I first heard "Bridge over Troubled Water," my mother popped into my mind and stayed there. *"When
you're weary / Feelin' small / When tears are in your eyes / I'll dry
them all / I'm on your side."* That summed up Mom perfectly.
I hummed that song often and played the words in my head
until I could hear them through the silence. When I closed my
eyes, my mother was always there to comfort me and dry my
tears. Always on my side.

My rap phase was in the early nineties, the tracksuit and
sideways cap era. I nearly wore out my cassette with "It Takes
Two" by Rob Base and DJ E-Z Rock after several years of playing it. I also listened to Sir Mix-a-Lot and, as embarrassing as

it is to say now, I cut more than my fair share of unimpressive dance-floor moves to "Baby Got Back."

On the other end of the spectrum, my friends and I used to camp at a state park where we'd hang out by picnic tables with a giant boom box playing "Free Bird" and "Tuesday's Gone" by Lynyrd Skynyrd. *"For I must be travelin' on now / 'Cause there's too many places I've got to see."* I remember looking out at the trees and the lake and thinking how wonderful it would be to live that kind of life, moving from town to town, *"'Cause I'm as free as a bird now / And this bird you'll never change."* The fact that we were five yards from my mom's minivan seemed irrelevant. The dream was all that mattered.

I later realized that all young men yearn for the road until they're on it. Then they realize why settlers ultimately settle. I also know now why "Free Bird" is on Skynyrd's first album and not their last. Even Ronnie and the boys realized that traveling day after day, being away from home and family night after night, can crush your soul. Still, those were songs I had to imprint on my brain, especially when I think back on how I felt as those guitars squalled and all the kids rocked back and forth to the beat.

As I hit the early and aggressive years of manhood, when invincibility and stupidity create a toxic stew, I listened to early U2, *Rattle and Hum* and *The Joshua Tree,* and realized that they made me see something new. *"I wanna run, I want to hide / I want to tear down the walls that hold me inside."* Hearing Bono belt those words for the first time told me that I was not alone. Other people, maybe all people, felt the same way I did. Some could even express it in a multiplatinum-selling song.

I wrote them all down on what was becoming a lengthy master list of music and lyrics that I had to memorize in more than a sing-along way. The playlist would become my mental gymnastics, the workout I needed to keep my brain sharp and my memories from my hearing life alive.

There were a few obscure ones. While at IU, a Dallas alternative rock and folk band called Jackopierce—a melding of the two guys' names—became popular on campuses everywhere. Ours was no exception. One spring break a big group of us went to South Padre Island, the only beach worth mentioning in Texas, where we slept eight guys to a room and lounged in the sand for a week. Jackopierce was playing a concert at a bar called Parrot Eyes (if you say it fast, you get the pun), and several of us arrived four hours early to get spots near the stage. Two hours later we were still the only people there, but we couldn't have cared less. It was worth it as we belted out the lyrics to "Vineyard" over one-dollar Lone Star beers. *"Won't you stay on the vineyard for the summer / Won't you stay on the vineyard for the year / We'll find a little house down there in Oak Bluffs / And our children is all that we hear."*

By the time I finished college, the Beatles were my band. I found them later than I should have, three decades after they broke up and at an age when I could appreciate the depth of words like *"There's a shadow hanging over me / Oh, yesterday came suddenly."* Thanks to friends with a musical spectrum broader than my own, at least I found them. From the reverb intro of "I Feel Fine" to the last note of "Get Back," I can remember the tight harmonies and rhythms echoing through the air. Their early stuff was essentially three chords and harmonizing the words "girl" and "love" in varying combinations. It was easy listening in the truest sense. Indiana offered a renowned class on the history of rock and roll, which was a prerequisite for the even more interesting "History of the Beatles." That class opened my mind to listening to the context in which music was written, the dynamics of the people and their times. That added a different dimension to the music for me. "Blackbird," for example, was written about racism. *"Blackbird singing in the dead of night / Take these broken wings and learn to fly."* *Rubber Soul* was a nod to those who thought the Beatles were faking their way into rock and jazz. "Octopus's Garden" is Ringo's interpretation of, well, wanting to visit an octopus's garden.

As I listened again and again with intense focus, some of the words of those songs spoke to me in ways they never had before. *"The long and winding road that leads to your door / Will never disappear, I've seen that road before."*

In 1966, Paul McCartney bought a 186-acre farm overlooking the Machrihanish Bay on the west coast of Scotland. There was a three-bedroom farmhouse that had been owned by a local farmer, Mr. Brown, and his wife, and a lone, narrow road leading in and out of the place—a long and winding one. I didn't know that story until recently. I just knew the song was beautiful when I could hear it, and heartwarming in a melancholy way when I almost couldn't. So many of my family relationships had been like that long and winding road. I wasn't special in that sense. Most kids don't recognize the unconditional love their parents show them until they are no longer under their wings. In my case, the lessons my dad taught my brother and me through his actions came back with every symphonic note of McCartney's three-minute-and-forty-second masterpiece. *"Don't leave me waiting here / lead me to your door."*

And then there is *"When I was younger, so much younger than today / I never needed anybody's help in any way / But now these days are gone / I'm not so self-assured"* or *"All my troubles seemed so far away / Now it looks as though they're here to stay / Oh, I believe in yesterday."* Spending time with those lyrics makes you see something more in music, in yourself, and in everyone around you.

Then there were the Nora songs, the ones that reminded me of all the moments with the partner I would have for life. At the time, I didn't think it would be possible to forget the Phish tunes we listened to as we held hands in those early weekends of romance. How could I forget how Beck sounded as I ran my fingers through Nora's hair? No way would I ever forget our toe-dipping into the Grateful Dead together. But I also knew that memory is a perishable asset. It has to be burnished on a regular basis. People who lose their hearing begin to speak in a different voice quickly because, without the auditory cues, they forget how they should sound. If I lost the sound of Sir Paul telling me how *"Rocky Raccoon went back to his room / only to find Gideon's Bible,"* more than music would be gone. I knew that I had to brand the songs of my soundtrack onto my frontal lobe. All of them.

It would be like learning to play an instrument or picking

up a foreign language, a methodical and often tedious task. But the memories that came with that music were worth every effort. The people—my parents, my brother, my friends, my teachers and coaches, and, of course, Nora—who connected me to those songs were all the motivation I needed.

SEVEN

*YOU'RE MY BLUE SKY, YOU'RE MY SUNNY DAY
LORD, YOU KNOW YOU MAKE ME HIGH WHEN YOU TURN
YOUR LOVE MY WAY.*

—The Allman Brothers Band

WE WERE MARRIED IN MUNSTER, INDIANA, NORA'S HOMETOWN, IN LATE OCTOBER OF 2002, A BEAUTIFUL, CRISP MIDWESTERN DAY WITH A SKY SO BLUE THE ALLMAN BROTHERS COULD HAVE SUNG ABOUT IT. As I waited at the altar of her church beside my groomsmen and a longtime friend who also happened to be the Methodist minister officiating the ceremony, I thought back on how we had come to this seminal stage in our lives.

For starters, most people knew this was coming long before

I did. I hadn't decided to pop the question to Nora yet when my mother, with a mixture of amusement and annoyance, told the story of how I had come out from under anesthesia after my surgery and, still groggy, asked for Nora instead of her or my dad, both of whom were waiting at my bedside. My folks had, of course, been supportive of our relationship from the beginning. They had seen a different spark in Nora, one far from the romantic weekends in Chicago or our rehab-room chats over popcorn and old movies. They saw a woman of substance and "sturdy stock," which are words my dad would have used and meant as high praise. They also saw a problem solver, a planner, a calm and devoted partner, someone who would bond our two families together rather than wedge them apart. They knew that I had made a wise choice.

Nora's parents were people I had grown to love more with each passing day, in part because they were so different from my folks. It's generally accepted science that overcoming obstacles is one of the driving forces of human nature. It is the nature of our being. Striving to overcome something is what gets us up in the morning. It gives life purpose. Why do you think people climb mountains? There are perfectly good aircraft to fly you over them. Or why do people who are not being chased by bears or trying to run down their food continue to get up early and run long distances as quickly as they can? They do it because humans need hurdles. We all need objectives that challenge us physically, mentally, and emotionally. It is what keeps mankind moving forward.

Winning the hearts and minds of Tom and Sarah Lasbury, Nora's parents, became my Everest. And in the weeks before our wedding, I had plenty of time to do it. Nora and I were buying a new apartment in the Wicker Park neighborhood of Chicago, a unit in a three-building complex that was under construction. Like most young couples at that time, we plunked all our savings into a down payment. I was lucky that, in the two years we dated, Nora had saved most of every paycheck. Her frugality and my meager contribution allowed us to qualify for a nicer place than most newlyweds our age could afford. Of course, when I showed the place to my parents, their first reaction was, "Too expensive." When we showed it to Tom and Sarah, Tom's first response was, "Is the unit upstairs available?" I told him that it was, but at a much greater cost. He said, "How much more?" When I gave him the number, he said, "That's not too much." He offered to loan us the difference at a rate we couldn't refuse. Turns out he was right. The upstairs unit had a patio with a view of the city. Once it was completed, we could have sold it immediately for a good deal more than what we paid.

Before that, though, we had to work through a few issues. When construction began, we were supposed to be handed the keys in August, a full eight weeks before taking our matrimonial vows. My plan was to have the furniture moved in, boxes unpacked, pictures hung, and dishes put away before Nora walked down the aisle. But as anyone who has ever built a house knows, everything takes twice as long and costs 50 percent more than you budgeted. It's one of those lessons that your parents know, but they let you learn on your own. Of course, being an eternal optimist (I am in marketing, after all), I timed the expiration of my apartment lease with the promised completion date. When the new place wasn't ready, I was homeless. Thankfully, Nora's mom, Sarah, refused to leave me on the street, so she let me live in their basement for a month, making the ninety-minute commute into the city each day until the house was ready. It was the same home where Nora grew up, walking distance from her school and near the Dairy Queen, a franchise that was the teen hangout in more than a few American small towns. During my time as a cellar dweller, sleeping on what felt like a medieval torture device disguised as a foldout sofa, I engaged in dinner conversations with Tom in a constant effort to make him believe I was worthy of stealing away his only child. We talked about the long-term value of good insurance, low mortgage rates, and high gas mileage. I also did the dishes and offered to help with anything they needed around the house before heading downstairs to my lair every night.

I wasn't quite sure what to make of Tom in the beginning. He had a dry wit that kept me off-kilter. Should I laugh at that last comment, or keep my mouth shut and chuckle later? He also had this knack of taking an extra beat before responding to anything. It couldn't have been more than a second, maybe two, but it felt like hours. I wanted to rush in with more verbal spasms to fill the painful vacuum of silence. What I didn't realize at the time, but would learn soon enough, was that Tom never uttered a syllable without having thought through the next paragraph or two. And he always measured the men around him against a high standard of ethics and decency. That was especially true of men who were getting close to the two most important women in his life: his wife and daughter.

After a few nights of eating lake perch (a northern Indiana delicacy), something about Tom clicked with me. He wasn't distant at all. In fact, he was interesting and funny, a man with an insatiable curiosity. He would come home with a gleam in his eye, eager to share whatever he'd learned that day. If the sun set without his knowing more than he did when it rose, Tom considered it a waste. He would constantly ask trivia questions—How long is a year on Mars? What is the deepest spot in the ocean? Which U.S. president is responsible for the word "okay," which is used in every Romance language to mean "things are fine"? (The answer to that last one is Martin Van Buren, who was from Kinderhook, New York, and was given the nickname "Old Kinderhook" by his colleagues in the Democratic Party, later shortened to OK.) Nothing seemed to be too obscure to escape Tom's knowledge. After a while, he would throw in a dollar or two if I knew how far the Earth was from the sun in September, or the name of the currency in Mozambique. Tom would later make a nice contribution to the Roth IRA he started for us when I correctly answered that lightning was responsible for more insurance claims per year than floods. But those conversations, and knowing that Africa has more landmass than North and South America combined, didn't calm my nerves when it came to asking for his daughter's hand in marriage.

I grew up in a generally conservative home and wasn't comfortable moving in with Nora (more accurately, it was suggesting this idea to her dad) without some serious commitment. So, in the small window of time between when Tom and I had started to connect and when the apartment decision needed to be made, I seized my moment. It was in Nora's childhood home, as I scrubbed a couple of pans next to an avocado-colored dishwasher, that I broached the subject of marriage. As the water ran in the sink, I thought about the first time I had met Sarah. She had taken Nora out to dinner to celebrate her earning a master's degree in hospital administration, and I had suggested that she drop her daughter off on a street corner outside of the Burwood Tap at 10:00 P.M. on a Friday night. Sarah had always given me more deference than I deserved. Just what Tom thought of that incident, or what I was thinking at the time, remain among life's greatest mysteries. But, standing in his kitchen, just as we were about the put the last dish away, I said to Tom, "I would like your permission, if you think it's okay, I mean, if you think it's a good idea . . . I'd like to ask marry to be my Nora . . . I mean . . . look . . . your daughter is my best friend and I'd like to spend the rest of my life with her."

This was followed by another of Tom's patented pauses, no more than a heartbeat—or three, since mine was racing at the time. Finally, he said, "Wellllll . . ." followed by another pause. Two pauses were never good. Two in one answer sent me into a flop sweat. One beat, two beats, and then, as if genuinely unsure, "I guess that would be okay."

I thought of that moment and more as I stared out at the 250 guests who had come in—some from the far reaches of the country—to share our wedding day. Getting married at age twenty-five meant that we still had friends from all stages of our lives: childhood pals we'd grown up with, college friends we thought would be friends forever, many of our colleagues from work, and, of course, lots of family. I looked over at No-ra's mom, proudly sitting in the second row with her sisters. When friends once asked me to describe my future mother-in-law, I answered that if personality was a blood type, Sarah was an O-positive, a universal donor of her time, talents, pa-tience, and parenting. I was already playing with house money having grown up with my own family, so adding the Lasburys (Tom, Sarah, and miles of cousins) was more than I probably deserved. As my eyes continued scanning the sanctuary, they ended with seeing Mom and Dad seated just a few feet away. I caught them both grinning. Of all the choices I'd made in my life—some good and many, many poor—Nora was the best in their minds.

When the wedding planner nodded and "Here Comes the Bride" kicked in on the piano, I stood a little straighter. Nora glowed from the moment she walked through the door. And Tom, who always walked with a cane because of his neurolog-ical condition, and because it was cool, had gone all out with a top hat and tails. But for the lack of a monocle, he looked like the dandy Eustace Tilley, the *New Yorker* mascot. Watch-ing him walk down the aisle, his cane in one hand and his daughter on the other, I thought about the day I took him to our townhome for the first time. He nodded, looked around, and said almost nothing until we got to the master bedroom. "Which one of you will sleep in here?" he asked.

The ceremony itself was traditional. We didn't write our own vows or break-dance down the aisle afterward, a craze that wouldn't come about for another decade, after the in-vention of social media. As many brides do, Nora referred to it as the best day of her life, which I knew meant that everything had been executed exactly as she'd planned. It was the perfect intersection of organization, budgeting, scripting, and decision-making, which was Nora's love language. Even the choice of day had been carefully crafted. That Saturday happened to be the day the clocks moved back from daylight saving to standard time, which meant we got an extra hour in the evening to celebrate with our friends.

Nora wrote the song list for the DJ at the reception. After the "now pronounce you man and wife" line and the pictures, but before the food, toast, cake, bouquet, and all the other punch-list items of a traditional wedding, the DJ pulled me aside and asked how much flexibility he had on the song list, "between one and ten, one being almost none and ten being pretty flexible," he said.

I answered, "Zero, man. She knows what she wants. And she put a lot of thought into this."

That's how it went. Dinner music was the soundtrack to the movie *I Am Sam*, with Sarah McLachlan's haunting version of "Blackbird" and Eddie Vedder's "You've Got to Hide Your Love Away"—*"Here I stand, head in hand / Turn my face to the wall / If she's gone, I can't go on / Feelin' two foot small."*

I concentrated through the conversations and the laughs to hear Sheryl Crow as she made "Mother Nature's Son" her own, and Rufus Wainwright, alone with his guitar, on "Across the Universe"—*"Jai guru deva om / Nothing's gonna change my world."*

In my mind, I added those versions to my soundtrack. When I played them in the silence, I wanted to remember John Lennon and Eddie Vedder, Paul McCartney and Sarah McLachlan. Separating the two would require discipline and practice, like learning my nines tables in elementary school. But if I could do it then, I could do it now.

As I looked around the room at all the people who had come to be with us, it dawned on me that this would never happen again. Friends I had kept close in my teens would build busy lives of their own with little time to keep in touch, much less to travel for a face-to-face meeting. Jobs would come and go in the future, for all of us, and with those changes the nature of our friendships would change. Even our families would evolve as we aged and grandparents, great-aunts, great-uncles, and eventually parents and cousins passed away. Never again would this eclectic gathering of friends be possible. I felt sure that even my funeral wouldn't attract this kind of outpouring.

My only regret was not taking the microphone. The social compact usually requires everyone to laugh at your jokes when you tell them at your wedding. I missed that opportunity. With so much going on, it didn't cross my mind until later. If I had grabbed the mic, I would have thanked Tom and Sarah for raising the most genuine and loving person I'd ever met, and I would have thanked them and my own parents for setting wonderful examples of what a marriage really means. Through their combined sixty years of experience passed along to us, Nora and I learned, through their example, the keys to successful long-term relationships. Love, as we felt it in that moment, would evolve. We knew that going in. Our parents showed us that persistence, partnership, and fighting through the rough patches that mark every marriage come down to a few simple but far-from-easy tasks. First, and perhaps most important, is kindness. Successful couples are kind to each other, even when they don't want to be, and even when one partner might not deserve it. Both sets of parents exhibited that trait.

They also showed us the value of the pause. Every marital interaction has the potential to go sideways if one of the parties speaks or acts quickly without considering the perspective of the other. That's where a pause becomes invaluable. Whether it's "Get up, the baby's crying," or "You forgot the garbage," or "I got a new job offer, we have to move," responding immediately can lead you both down a rocky road, one that will hurt your feet and feelings long after the circumstances that led to your response pass. It sometimes drove me nuts to sit through the silent gaps in my parents' discussions. In my youthful mind, I thought I had the perfect quip for every occasion. What Nora and I learned is that a biting retort might make you feel good in the moment, but the damage it causes will haunt you for a long time. The words you share can create hope, patience, and a deep and abiding love, or they can sow discord and turmoil, anger and resentment. Taking a breath to think of the other party before answering is a trait found in many if not most successful marriages.

Neither set of parents would admit it, but they also taught us the value of a loving stubbornness, of not giving up or giving in on your relationship. If I'd taken the mic that night, I would have thanked my parents, Ken and Linda, for having the foresight to let Mom show me all the right things to do in a marriage, and Dad show me all the wrong. And while the guests would have laughed, they would have known that there is a kernel of truth in all comedy, but Mom meant everything to Dad and vice versa.

The soundtrack from our reception could have come out of any romantic movie of the last two decades. Michael Jackson and Kool & the Gang—"*Celebrate good times, come on*"—had everybody hopping. We also yelled lyrics along with Neil Diamond—"*Sweet Caroline . . . bah, bah, bah*"—and slow-danced to Billy Joel—"*I want you just the way you are.*" There were a couple of offbeat ones. My family wasn't thrilled with the 2Pac numbers, but Dad cut a rug to Kenny Rogers. Nora and I both smiled at the irony of singing Elvis to each other—"*We can't go on together, with suspicious minds.*"

We used every minute of our extra Central Standard Time hour to enjoy the day and night together. The last song was "Baba O'Riley" by the Who, so my wedding reception ended with all my friends yelling, "*We're all wasted.*"

Then Nora and I rode away from the crowd gathered outside. I looked at their beaming faces and told myself to never forget the feelings from this moment, not just because I was entering a new phase of life as a married man, but because all these people would probably never be assembled again. This snapshot of our personal history would fade in the winds of time. Like the songs of my life, it was up to me to preserve them. "*Misty watercolor memories of the way we were.*"

EIGHT

HERE COMES THE SUN, AND I SAY, IT'S ALL RIGHT.

—George Harrison

DON'T KNOW WHAT I EXPECTED, BECAUSE LIKE ANY LOOMING LOSS, YOU TRY TO SHOVE IT INTO THE CELLAR OF YOUR MIND. But I certainly didn't expect that George Harrison's "Here Comes the Sun" would be the last song I heard with my own ears. *"Little darling, it's been a long, cold, lonely winter."*

George wrote those words in Eric Clapton's garden early in 1969, after a brutal English winter. I can still hear the harmonies with John in the background, *"Sun, sun, sun, here it comes."* At its most superficial, the song is about welcoming a new day. At a deeper level, it is about rebirth and renewal. The Beatles had gone through a difficult stretch after the death of their manager, Brian Epstein, before the *Abbey Road* album was released. George was trying to capture his feelings on the band coming out of that darkness, on the changing seasons of life, and on how hardships make us appreciate brighter times. For me, that Wednesday morning in August, with George crooning away—"*Little darling, I feel the ice is slowly melting*"—certainly marked a new phase.

Nora and I had nestled into home life in our wonderful neighborhood. I often read the newspaper, the actual print edition of the *Chicago Sun-Times*, on our rooftop deck with a cup of coffee and a view of the skyline, the points on the Willis Tower jutting up against the rising sun. We were having some of Nora's family over for lunch, a celebration of our new place. We were both looking forward to some midday entertaining. I didn't come home for lunch often, so this was looking like a treat for everyone.

Something else was different that morning. We had a westerly wind off Lake Michigan, and our unit sat a mile west of the Blommer Chocolate Company. On the days when we got this breeze, it smelled like we lived inside a Yankee candle.

Everything else seemed routine. We lay in bed for a few minutes after the seven fifteen alarm and listened to the end of George's song: "*It's all right*," followed by a G chord, D to F sharp, E minor, E minor 7, and A7. "*It's all right*," and the last chords I would ever hear—F, C, G / B, G, and a perfect capstone D. If you're going to end your natural hearing with a classic, there are few better. Of course, I didn't know at the time that I wouldn't hear another song the same way, which is the opposite of most things in life. More often than not, you remember firsts, not lasts—first dates, first kisses, first cars, the first time you spoke in public—but you rarely realize at the time that you are doing something for the final time. Everyone knows that Neil Armstrong was the first man on the moon. Few remember that Gene Cernan was the last. The only lasts we remember involve heartbreak. You recall the last thing said when a relationship dissolves, and you will never forget the last moments you shared with your parents before they passed away. Those "last things" in life linger, because you miss them. I guess losing my hearing fit that bill.

My twenty-five-year-old life had been far from extraordinary at that point, which is exactly how I wanted it. In my mind, I had married the most wonderful woman on the planet and lived in the best city in world. My job was great, and our families were happy. There was that niggling problem of recurring brain tumors, but I treated my hearing like any other skill that I couldn't quite master. I was good at creating presentations and public speaking, but I was not a great guitarist or painter. I could fly-fish with the best of them, and I was still healthy and driven enough to run marathons, but I danced like a windup toy, and I would have been a lousy contestant on *The Great British Baking Show*. By compartmentalizing my hearing loss this way—accentuating the positives and working around the negatives—I felt as though I had done quite well. When I was going through the job-interview process, I set up in-person meetings in quiet, low-traffic places. Nonchain coffee shops at 2:00 P.M. worked great. I would also do video calls whenever possible, and nothing about my hearing loss stopped me from building a PowerPoint deck. Hearing was just something I didn't do well, like painting, or sailing, or riding a horse.

Knowing this day would ultimately come, I had spent time

preparing for my hearing to take *"that midnight train to Georgia."* Nora and I had taken a few American Sign Language lessons, but to the shock of absolutely no one who knew us, she was much better at it than I. By the time she had the entire alphabet memorized, I had learned to sign "I love you" and "cool," which I figured would get me out of most situations.

My playlist had shaped up by then, as well, and I had polished my memorization techniques. If you listen to a song several times while intermittently turning the volume up and down, you can play it in your mind in the spots where you aren't hearing. If the mental version matches up to the musicians' when you turn the volume back up, you know you've memorized the tempo. I did that several times a day. Then I would hum the note and sing the words in my mind. Randy Jackson and Simon Cowell would have called my singing "pitchy," but performance was not the point. Just as reciting poetry aloud is more for you than anyone who might be listening, my singing was about memorization and immersion, not winning a talent show.

Picking out instrumental parts was a little tougher. A good producer will blend every instrument to create one seamless sound. As a memorizer, I had to isolate those tracks in my mind, then put them back together. You start with the beat of a drum, then follow the syncopation. Then you listen for the single lick, be it on a guitar or keyboard, that drives the melody. Once you hear them separately, it's a treat to meld them into one sound in your mind.

The same was true with vocal harmonies. Remembering the melody of a song is like watching only one player at a time on a basketball court—you can follow the ball, but you miss the beauty of the teamwork. I isolated the vocal tracks in my mind by humming each part as I played the songs over and over. Journey—"*Ooh, the wheel in the sky keeps on turnin' / Don't know where I'll be tomorrow.*" The Black Crowes—"*She says she talks to angels / Said they call her out by name.*" The acoustic guitar in that one struck me when I was in high school, but it wasn't until I graduated from college that I learned Chris and Rich Robinson wrote "She Talks to Angels" about the heroin-addicted girls they knew from the club scene in Atlanta. Learning that made it sadder and more profound. You want to reach out to the fictional girl in that song and rescue her from that "*smile when the pain comes.*"

We all need rescuing every now and again.

On a lighter note, I memorized Prince's version of "Kiss"—"*You don't have to be rich / to be my girl / You don't have to be cool / to rule my world,*" although I hummed it an octave lower, more in line with the Tom Jones version.

Johnny Cash turned out to be easier to remember than I'd imagined. I could close my eyes, imagine the chattering wheels of a freight train, and find the rhythm—"*I fell into a burning ring of fire / I went down, down, down, and the flames grew higher.*"

But some of the most difficult songs were the ones with the simplest lyrics. "*I was shaking at the knees / Could I come again please? / Yeah, the ladies were too kind / You've been thunderstruck.*" In addition to all the innuendo and double entendre, the memorable thing about AC/DC was the guitar parts. Most people know "Thunderstruck," "Back in Black," and "Rock and Roll Ain't Noise Pollution" long before the first note is sung. One riff and people are bopping their heads and raising a fist in the air. You lose that in the silence. I can close my eyes and hear Brian Johnson drawing on a cigarette and saying, *"Hey there, all you middlemen / Throw away your fancy clothes,"* but I can never hear Angus Young's power chords in my mind like I could through my ears.

Sometimes, I could cue my brain with a sound or two. I could whistle like Axl Rose in the opening bars of "Patience," and then imagine every acoustic progression that followed. *"Said sugar, make it slow and we'll come together fine / All we need is just a little patience."*

I also memorized some of the most overplayed songs of a generation, all of which sparked memories. I wasn't alive in 1969, but I could certainly hear Bryan Adams singing, *"I got my first real six-string / Bought it at the five and dime / Played it 'til my fingers bled / Was the summer of '69."* What the heck is a five and dime? Oh, well, that didn't matter. I loved the feelings songs like that rekindled. I even memorized "Eye of the Tiger" by Survivor. *"Went the distance, now I'm back on my feet / Just a man and his will to survive."*

Calling my list eclectic would be kind. One second I would be tapping my toes 137 beats per minute and humming "Eleanor Rigby" in E minor, and the next I would slow the tap down to 108 and shift to A flat major for a little Stevie Wonder. *"Boogie on reggae woman / What is wrong with me? / Boogie on reggae woman / Baby can't you see."*

I could seamlessly slide from "Three Little Birds" by Bob Marley to "If I Had a Million Dollars" by Barenaked Ladies, and then just straight into some down-home country cookin' with Kenny Rogers, *"Everyone considered him the coward of the county / He'd never stood one single time to prove the county wrong."*

Bob Dylan's version of "Mr. Tambourine Man" wasn't the most melodic. That title probably belonged to the Byrds, who covered Dylan's song a year after he wrote it. You can find twenty versions that are more musically sound than the original. Judy Collins covered it; so did the Lettermen, Chad and Jeremy, and the Four Seasons. Even William Shatner recorded a spoken-word version in 1968. But I loved Dylan's original, with all his sliding pitches and folksy strums. That was the version I embedded into my brain.

Somehow, I could go from there straight to the perfect harmonies of Glenn Frey and Don Henley wailing a Jackson Browne song—*"Well, I'm standing on a corner in Winslow, Arizona / Such a fine sight to see."* It said a lot about America that a band known as the heart and soul of the California sound could be led by two guys from Detroit, Michigan, and Linden, Texas, but if Glenn and Don could reinvent themselves, why couldn't the rest of us? And if those guys got second and third chances at life, and a guy like glam-rocker Bret Michaels— "Every Rose Has Its Thorn"—could keep himself relevant two decades after his last hit, why couldn't a young man with hearing loss do the same in the land of opportunity?

The morning I lost my hearing, I put on my best three-button suit and the Brooks Brothers tie I had bought for my college graduation. This wardrobe choice wasn't just because we were having guests. That was part of it. But, also, News America

Marketing remained the last vestige of old-school dress codes in the country. While most of my old fraternity brothers went to work in khakis and polo shirts four days a week and then put on jeans and a jersey for casual Fridays, I thought I worked at the last non-law-firm business in the country that required everyone to wear a suit and tie every day. I didn't mind. In fact, I liked it. I was twenty-five and looked fourteen. The clothes at least kept clients from thinking I was there for Bring Your Kid to Work Day.

After coffee and the smell of chocolate wafting in from the west, I made my traditional walk to the Division Street Blue Line, a train that would take me within a block of my office.

The morning was unremarkable in every way other than reminding everyone in the office of the afternoon I had planned. I was still a cubicle guy, one of many young, eager, first-job professionals in a marketing department, so it was incumbent upon me to let everyone know why I was taking a longer-than-normal lunch break. We normally got an hour. The commute home was thirty minutes one way. I was not in a position to dictate how long I could be away, so I communicated my intentions up, down, and across the chain of command.

At noon, I grabbed my jacket and tightened my tie, tucked in the tail of my dress shirt, and ran my hands down the lapels of my suit coat to smooth out any wrinkles from the day. As I entered the elevator, I looked at myself in the brass doors, making sure the dimple in my Windsor knot was just right. The elevator was full, which was not unusual for that time of day. People in office buildings tend to vacate at noon, whether or not they have lunch plans. Plus, our office was connected to a Hyatt that hosted a lot of international conferences. It would have been surprising if the elevator wasn't packed.

What caught me off guard, though, was the sound, or lack thereof. I was accustomed to hearing a lot of people talk at once, the way you might hear kids in the deep end of a swimming pool—a muffled, garbled, and indecipherable racket—but if I concentrated, I could almost always pick out a word or two, maybe a phrase that I could use as a clue. By latching on to one thread, I could usually piece together what these strangers were saying. Most people think of that as eavesdropping. The hearing challenged view it as a test. Could I assemble enough scraps of information, a syllable here, a delivery there, to cobble together a story?

This time, I could not. After not picking up a single intelligible word, I decided that my elevator companions must be conference attendees from the hotel who were speaking a foreign language. Again, I was looking at the blurry stop sign and assuming the guy who painted it must have been having a bad day. But the sounds I heard on that elevator sounded like Albanian or Farsi, anything but good old Midwestern English. They had to be foreign. It was, I assumed, the only logical explanation.

Because of time constraints, I took a cab home. This was before the days of rideshares, a time when you actually had to stand on a street corner with your hand in the air and hope a cabdriver saw you. It was also a time in my life when I counted all my pennies. A cab ride was a luxury I rarely afforded myself, but this was a special occasion. A nice gentleman in a yellow cab did, indeed, pick me up, but when he spoke to me, I couldn't understand anything he said. An awkward pause followed. In my mind, I blamed the driver, which wasn't totally unfair. Most people in Chicago were lucky to catch half of what a cabbie said through the Plexiglas partition. When he said something that sounded like a whale song, "Wr'oooo," I correctly guessed that he was asking "Where to?" so I gave him my address.

I read the rest of the newspaper on the ride, in part because I always liked to keep up with the news, and I enjoyed good writing, but also to keep the driver from making any unnecessary conversation. Nothing says "We're not chatting" like a newspaper over your face.

Nora's family was already at our place when I got home. Tom was on the rooftop looking toward the city and no doubt taking great satisfaction in his investment. He also wore a tie, not because of an office dress code, but because he was the kind of man who would dress up to visit his daughter and her new husband in their first home. In his mind, this was a celebration, which meant dressing the part.

I still had trouble understanding anyone at lunch. It had to be that westerly chocolate-infused wind putting gremlins in my hearing aids, or so I told myself, another mysterious lie that my psyche kept passing off as the truth. I struggled through lunch and then cut out after the meal and a few pictures. Everyone had a great time, an afternoon to remember, or so I thought.

Later Nora told me her mother was perplexed by my unwillingness to make small talk. I had seemed aloof and distracted. Even Nora thought I had copped an attitude when she yelled down at me from the roof as I got into another cab. She watched as I closed the door without looking up.

I arrived back at the office and rode back up twenty-one floors, only this time, my manager hopped on with me. He smiled and said something that I missed. That wasn't a big deal. It happened a lot. I had mastered the art of asking people to repeat themselves in as many polite ways as possible. Say again? How's that? Pardon? One more time? I didn't catch that last part.

My manager was used to it as well, so he smiled and repeated himself. Only the words sounded like Charlie Brown's teacher from the old cartoons—"*Womwomwom, wowumwum.*" I could see his mouth moving, but the tones coming out were like an underwater trombone. We were in an elevator, inches from each other, and I couldn't pick up a single word. For the first time all day I thought, This is not good.

I nodded and read his face, the instincts kicking in from elementary school days. I read his facial expressions and tried to figure out if I should smile, nod, or look contemplative. My mind raced. It was one thing to bluff an elementary school nurse or your college fraternity brothers, but this was next-level scary. The elevator ride seemed to take forever. Out of things to say and ways to compensate, I took out my hearing aid and studied it like it was the Rosetta Stone. "I'm sorry," I said to my boss. "My battery must have died." When the elevator doors finally opened, I almost sprinted to my cubicle.

"Breathe, Matt, it's probably nothing," I said to myself. Whether or not those words came out of my mouth or I just thought them was a mystery, because I couldn't hear myself. I grabbed a spare battery and put it into my hearing aid. There were a series of self-tests that I had become practiced at running, S's and T's to make sure the hearing aid was working. "Ssssssss . . . Shshshshshsh . . . Tutututututu . . . Tatatatata." Instead of hearing the crisp sounds that had always followed a battery change, I got nothing but dull thuds. Well, that's new, I told myself while trying not to hyperventilate. The hearing aid appeared to be working as it should, but my brain wasn't accepting sounds. At first, I thought I might be having a stroke. Can you self-diagnose that? I wasn't sure, so I did some multiplication problems in my head. I made a fist and then stretched my fingers out, first with my right hand and then my left. I touched my nose—left hand and then right— and then I untied and retied my shoes. I did that with my eyes open and then tried it with my eyes closed. That last experiment failed, but tying your shoelaces with your eyes closed is harder than it sounds, so I gave myself a pass on that one.

When you look back on how you reacted in the midst of a crisis, there are always things you think you should have done, or things you did that you realize were silly. Self-diagnosing a stroke is not sound medical advice. If you think you or anyone around you is having a stroke, don't waste time conducting random cognitive tests. Call 911 and get medical assistance immediately. The other thing you should do, first and foremost, is call your spouse, especially if she is a former med student with a clinician's knowledge of your condition.

It took longer than it should have for me to call Nora. When I did, I didn't know what to say at first, so I just blurted out, "Hey, I think it's happening. I think this is it."

I had to assume she knew what "it" was. I also have to assume that the news caused her to pause and reflect before speaking, because I have no idea if she responded or not. She could have offered brilliant advice or a calming, inspirational message, but I didn't hear a word of it.

After a quick explanation to my boss and coworkers that I was having a "medical issue" and needed to go—again, not something you discuss often at work, and I had no idea how they responded since I couldn't hear them—I rode the same elevator back down and got into another cab. It was my third cab ride of the day and the first where I didn't think about the cost. The only thing sadder to me at that moment than losing my hearing was doing so seated next to a stranger on public transportation. If this was, indeed, it, I wanted to be alone or with Nora. Getting home fast was all that mattered now.

What do you do when faced with an unsolvable problem? What happens when circumstances are beyond your control and you must face an inevitable outcome with no recourse or answers? People have been asking that question as long as humans have existed. A drought turns your farmland into a dust bowl, and you are faced with starvation. How do you respond to that? What do you say to those who count on you for their survival? What do you do when your home and family are swept away in a flood? How do men and women handle hardships they cannot control, tragedy they cannot change, or hurdles they cannot clear? We all like to believe that we would be noble heroes in the face of certain doom, that we would all be King Leonidas leading the three hundred Spartans into history at Thermopylae.

The truth is, you don't know until you are there, until you face that tiger and look him in the eye. As much as we would like to think we would be the fearless warrior, those people who do miraculous and heroic things will tell you that they were scared to death and just did their jobs anyway. From Moses leading the Israelites out of Egypt to the Okie fathers packing up the pickup truck and taking their families west through the desert in the depths of the Great Depression, people do what circumstances demand. And in most instances, they are petrified by fear the entire way.

I often describe losing my hearing as being like falling in a bottomless pit. In the beginning the sensation and the knowledge of what's happening are terrifying. But after three or four years, waking up in a free fall seems normal. You tend to almost forget that you are falling, because it becomes your day-to-day routine. Despite all the years that I had known this day was coming, I had been able to push it aside. It was the steamroller that kept chugging toward me, but as long as it was still in the distance, I could put it out of mind.

That had become harder to do as my hearing got worse. Where I had once been able to fake it till I made it in most settings, the deterioration of my hearing had robbed me of more than a means of communication. Personal connections had always been an integral part of who I was. At parties, I was the guy who remembered your girlfriend's name and asked how your brother was doing in his new job. I was the guy who complimented your mother on her beautiful earrings and shook your father's hand with both of mine. Hearing loss changed that. Now, it looked like my interactions with the outside world would be altered forever.

I remember a neurosurgeon once told me, "You're going to lose your hearing, but in the grand scheme of things, it's not a big a deal." I know he meant well. There are greater priorities to worry about when you have NF2, survival being at the top of the list, but that statement was obviously coming from someone who was not losing his hearing. In the moment, losing your hearing is an enormous deal, a giant, devastating, all-consuming deal. A new season of life was upon us. And while I had no choice but to face the day with courage and conviction, the feelings as I sat in the back of that cab were unmistakable. I was scared.

The steamroller had finally reached me, big and heavy and unrelenting.

The cabdriver stopped in front of our house and said something to me that I could not understand. I took the three flights of steps two at a time to get to our place, the one we had been celebrating just a couple of hours before. Nora was standing at the top of the landing waiting on me. Seeing her hit me like a wave. Her life was about to change again, and, as always, all she thought about was me, my well-being and my feelings. I had to catch myself to keep from crying, not at my loss but at my good fortune. She deserved an apology, and I almost said, "I'm sorry." I was stuck with the brain I'd been given at birth, but she had entered this life by choice. She stood there, her head tilted slightly, with a closed-lipped smile, a look I had come to know meant, "This is a tough day, but we will get through it together." When I got to the landing, she held out her hand, her forefinger and pinky up and her thumb out to the side. It was the American Sign Language symbol for "I love you," one of the few signs I'd managed to learn.

We hugged and went inside. I have no idea if she said anything in those first moments, but I knew that she was not only an advocate, she was my champion. If our time together had taught me anything, it was that when struggles hit, we pulled closer. The routine moments of life were when we operated almost as business partners, but when challenged, we put everything aside for each other. Never was that more obvious than the day I lost my natural hearing for good.

Once inside, I could hold it no longer. Tears rolled down my cheeks and into the corners of my mouth, their warm, salty taste only increasing the flow. I took a few deep breaths and tried to steel myself. This wasn't a pity party. I cried for the hardship I had foisted onto my beautiful wife. Even though she and I had always known this day was coming, I still envisioned myself as a provider and caretaker, all the things a man feels he should be once he starts a family. Not only did I feel that I had let my wife down, I felt that I was somehow less of a man.

Nora must have sensed what I was feeling as she held me. Without releasing her grip, she leaned back where I could see her lips and said, "Matt, we'll deal with this and be okay. I don't need a protector. I don't need a provider. I don't need a caretaker. I need you to be you." Because of all the time we had spent together, I could read her lips well, even though the sounds were fading fast.

Realizing that I was understanding, she continued. "We knew this day was coming. We planned for it. It's probably going to be weird having to make constant eye contact when we argue, but we'll figure that out, too. But we know what we need to do. We'll call the ENT and the House Ear Institute and get you checked and scheduled to have that brainstem implant they said might help. Then we'll call your HR people and get things sorted out at work. Then I will let our families know. But all that will start tomorrow. Right now, we're going to Adobo Grill for margaritas."

Tequila might have seemed cavalier given the events of the moment, but it was the perfect answer. Going out for a drink proved that our lives, our marriage, and the things we held dear would continue. Life would be different. We both had prepared for that, but at least we knew that we had each other.

We changed out of our work clothes. I carefully hung the suit and tie back in the closet, not knowing when I would wear them again. Then we walked three blocks to Division Street, the part of our neighborhood that had what Chicagoans called an "up-and-coming" restaurant scene. I had my right hand in my pocket, and Nora looped her arm into mine as we walked in matching strides. This was how we had walked throughout our relationship because my left ear was already shot by the time we started dating. We called my right my "good ear," although that was like calling a 1972 Pinto "the good car" because it was not up on blocks with the engine missing. We loved this part of town, but this time, we walked in silence because walking and talking were not things we could do at the same time at that point. I needed to see lips move, which was impossible if I was walking beside Nora on a busy street. Plus, we had a lot on our minds. We were both building lists of the things we needed to share before my hearing window closed for good. This was our one last chance to do things together in this world.

Adobo Grill, our favorite spot in the area, was a good place to start. We grabbed an outdoor table and watched a parade of people, many smiling and laughing as they chatted with each other. I saw a woman nodding as she looked ahead, a friend on her right telling an animated story. I wondered what they were saying, and I felt sad again for the fact that eavesdropping was probably a thing of the past.

Our server arrived and Nora ordered for the both of us, the first of a thousand tiny cuts. Adobo was the spot that had changed my mind about margaritas. I had always thought of them as punch bowl drinks for sorority girls. But this place did the traditional margarita better than anywhere in the city, and they coupled it with tableside guacamole where we could provide input into the saltiness and spiciness to suit our tastes. The drinks came and the server left the big bowl of guacamole and chips on the table. It would have been the perfect date had it not been for the going deaf thing that had happened earlier.

"I love you," I said to Nora, and for the moment, I let the day, the city, and the rest of the world slip away in the summer breeze. This wasn't a throwaway "I love you," not the kind you say before you hang up the phone or as you're walking out the door on your way to work; not an "I'll pick up dinner on the way home, I love you" kind of thing. I poured out the words as if it would be the last time they came out of my mouth, out of my heart and my soul. I didn't want her to hear me. I wanted her to feel what I felt.

"Matt, I love you, too. I love you. I'm here for you. We'll get through this. I love you."

I leaned in a little closer, smiled, and said, "What'd you say?"

In that moment, I wasn't about to pass up an opportunity for a deaf joke.

She laughed, which I actually heard, or I think I did. Memory is a tricky thing. You can believe you are hearing something because you know it's happening, and you have heard it so many times before that your mind plays the soundtrack for you. Nora had gradations of laughter. There was the polite laugh at a joke she didn't really find funny. Then there was the "that's actually pretty funny" laugh that makes the person who provoked it feel good. But this one was the "that's really funny and I'm so happy right now" laugh, the one that turned heads and brightened the mood of everyone who heard her. It was an expression of uninhibited joy that included head bobbing and a snort or two, followed by a big inhale and an attempt to wipe away tears. Her laugh could sell tickets.

I will forever miss hearing the Beatles with my own ears. But in that moment, I wanted to study Nora's laugh, memorize and store it for instant recall whenever I saw her mouth open and her head pitch forward in a chortling gasp.

"What do you see when you turn out the lights / I can't tell you, but I know it's mine / Oh, I get by with a little help from my friends."

We sat there for hours laughing through tears of joy, sadness, and a tinge of fear. We joked about a future of burned pizza and missed alarm clocks. I promised not to burn the house down, which was funny only because it was a legitimate concern. We laughed at the good news that I would never again have to hear Phil Collins sing "I Can't Dance." And we held hands and commented on the underrated nature of good tequila. Occasionally our server would wheel the guacamole cart by the table and wonder why this lovely girl was yelling such sweet things to that boy.

It was a moment we will both cherish for the rest of our lives.

The next day, I woke up in a world of silence—no alarm clock; no soft groan next to me as Nora pulled herself out of darkness and into the day; no sound of water from the shower; no bubbling from the coffee machine as the pot brewed or exhaling hiss as the last drops found their home; no hum of an electric toothbrush, and weirdest of all, no sound when I spoke. I could no longer hear myself, which terrified me. Was I yelling? Was I whispering? Was I pronouncing words I'd used all my life in a way that others understood? I opened the door that led to the terrace facing the street and noticed that I couldn't hear it close behind me. That's when I realized that there would be no way for me to know if someone came into or out of our house. I wouldn't hear a door close, wouldn't hear footsteps, wouldn't hear a bump or a bang if they hit a counter or knocked something onto the floor. That feeling left me cold and paranoid. What precautions could I make to warn me that someone was at the door?

I saw cars, even the occasional truck on the roads near our place, but there was no sound. It was as if I had gone to sleep on one planet and awakened on another. I had always had the confidence and courage to play whatever hand I'd been dealt. But now I didn't know the rules of the game.

Hard of hearing had been difficult, but totally deaf was scarier than I had imagined. You can walk through your house with the lights off, because there's ambient light somewhere, even if it's from the stars peeking in between your blinds. Your eyes can pick up something. If you've ever been in a cave with no light, you know that the feeling is a lot more frightening. I didn't panic—when you've had years to prepare for something, you'd like to think you have the strength not to fall to pieces when it happens—but I felt my heart rate quicken. The only thing I wanted to do at that moment was say "I love you" to myself over and over, not in my voice, but in Nora's. It had been only a day, but the thought of losing those words terrified me. I had tried to prepare myself, but how do you get ready for sound to go from being a sense to a memory?

Then I sang a couple of the songs on my list, just to fill my brain with the sounds my ears could no longer hear. *"It's the eye of the tiger / it's the thrill of the fight."* Not this time. It was impossible to convince myself that I had anything approaching a tiger's eye in this situation. Because as much as the apex predator kept a killer look on his face, he would also hear where his enemy and prey were lurking. Removing the sense of hearing tended to drain your confidence, tiger or not.

It wasn't supposed to be a surprise, and it certainly wasn't supposed to be this depressing. Turns out "The Sound of Silence" isn't a sound at all; it's a weight on your shoulders and a vise around your chest. Paul Simon got part of the song right. The day you wake up deaf, you say hello to darkness, but he is anything but an old friend. *"'Fools,' said I, 'You do not know / Silence like a cancer grows.'"*

The inevitable had become reality. At least for me, as Paul and Artie said, *"My words, like silent raindrops, fell / and echoed in the wells of silence."*

In my mind I knew it was time to get to work. But in my heart and soul, another song, by another guy named Paul, kept coming back to the surface. Instinctively, I knew I had to keep my playlists separate. I had to show discipline when remembering the songs or they would become a jumbled mess in my brain. Still, I jumped from one Paul to another, even though I couldn't hear myself humming the song that now consumed me.

"Suddenly I'm not half the man I used to be / There's a shadow hanging over me / Oh, yesterday came suddenly."

NINE

YOUR CANDLE BLEW OUT LONG BEFORE
YOUR LEGEND EVER DID

—Elton John

TEN DAYS LATER, LIFE THREW A SLEDGEHAMMER AT OUR HEADS. We had spent days researching surgical options for an auditory brainstem implant and reading the history and science of the process. The digital hearing aids that had been implanted during my junior year of college had, at the time, been temporarily miraculous, so good that they made me believe I could outrun the inevitable. Now that dream was over. Nora and I had spent a week looking through insurance policies and having meetings with the human resources department at my job. The night of August 28, we came in off the rooftop deck and were playing a game of Scrabble, one of our favorite pastimes, since it was a way to use words without speaking. Nora was about to rack up a huge score with the word "totality" when the phone rang. The only way I knew the phone rang was when Nora answered it. It was her mom, Sarah, and everything changed.

Sarah had called earlier to say that Tom had not come home yet, which was a little unusual, but not too concerning. Tom was a consummate tinkerer. He loved collecting gadgets and figuring out how they worked. For as long as I had known him, and, according to Nora, for most of her life, business suits were his everyday attire. He always carried an envelope in one of the breast pockets of his jacket and he would jot notes, trivia, and other tidbits of information and keep them there. He would pull them out and say things like, "Did you know that the expression 'if the Good Lord's willing and the creek don't rise' isn't a bad-grammar allusion to a flood? It's about the Creek Indians. 'If the Good Lord's willing and there isn't a Native American uprising.'" He loved stuff like that, it didn't matter much to him if it was true or not. When he didn't have a nugget to share, he would play tic-tac-toe on the envelope. Nora had no idea how many games they had played over the years, but it was in the thousands.

He was also an early adopter of technology, a beta tester before many people knew what that meant. Tom had just bought a new nautical GPS device and wanted to give it a try, so that Saturday he rented a boat and went out on a small lake in northwestern Indiana, not to test his sailing skill but to give his new gizmo a run. When he didn't come home at the prescribed time, Sarah began to worry.

It stormed around sundown. The people who rented Tom the boat became concerned. They could see it—the lake wasn't that big—but they couldn't see any movement. Not long afterward, a group near the shore saw what appeared to be a man in the water. They rushed out and pulled Tom ashore, attempting to revive him on the spot.

Late that night, as we were preparing for bed, Sarah called again. We needed to meet her at St. Anthony Medical Center in Crown Point, Indiana. Sarah's next words were, "He didn't make it."

I didn't have to hear the words to know what had happened. Seeing shock and grief wash over Nora like a giant wave didn't require sound. In the course of just over a week, my wife had lost the husband she had known to that point, and now she had lost her father forever. The fact that the last day I heard with my own ears would also be the last day we saw Tom only exacerbated the overwhelming sense of heartbreak. He had been so charming that day at our lunch, buttoned up and dapper with his coat and his cane, ready to admire his daughter, her new husband, and the home he'd helped us procure. I, of course, had shown up deaf and harried, unsure what was happening and unable to hold up my end of the social contract. I'm sure there were many awkward moments that afternoon that were my fault. I still regret what I didn't know at the time. The memory of that day had just become harder. The lasts in life always are.

I wanted to carry Nora's sadness, to lighten at least some of the load for my best friend. Her father had adored and protected her in ways I could not understand at the time. Nora inherited the best traits of both parents. She looked a lot like

Tom in the best possible ways. I saw a lot of him in her wry smile and the way she would raise her eyebrows in a quick little wave, almost a wink in reverse. Her curiosity came from him. There was no subject Tom didn't find fascinating. He devoured books, sometimes reading them cover to cover in one sitting, and he always walked away with more questions to be researched and answered. The internet, which was still young when we lost him, was the invention he assumed would enlighten the world. No longer would a question like "How long did it take to build the Empire State Building?" require digging an old Britannica encyclopedia off the shelf or making a phone call to a researcher. Tom thought the world would become smarter because we had the Library of Alexandria at our fingertips. I think he would be disappointed to see technology used to post dancing cat videos on TikTok.

Nora is the same way. She remains fascinated by the way things work. That is her father made over. It is also one of the reasons she majored in biology and went to a year of medical school. The challenge of solving problems, illuminating the unknowns, and bringing new ideas to life were instilled into her early.

She also enjoys the occasional Hershey bar, which was a throwback to her childhood and visiting Tom in his insurance office. He would put his daughter in his lap and say, "Does Mommy love Nora?" Of course, she would answer, "Yes." Then he would say, "Does Daddy love Nora?" That, too, was followed by her saying, "Yes." Then he would ask, "Does Nora love Nora?" At first, that one threw her. But as Tom continued to ask the question and Nora continued to answer, "Yes," she slowly realized that the affirmation of loving yourself was an important part of loving others. Once they had gone through that ritual, Tom would open the desk drawer and pull out a chocolate bar for each of them. He was always a sucker for a good dessert, or sometimes two. I only knew him for a few years, but the Tom stories have lasted decades, his candle certainly blew out long before the legend.

Our home was about an hour from the hospital, one of the longest rides of our lives. Nora had to drive. Being deaf does not keep you from getting a driver's license, but the tumors growing on my nerves were causing balance issues, which presents a problem on the road. It turns out, equilibrium is essential to operating a two-ton vehicle at a high rate of speed. Once more, I couldn't step up and help my wife in her darkest hour. We also couldn't talk in the car. Sign language and lipreading were all I had at that point, neither of which worked since Nora had her eyes on the road and her hands on the wheel.

The emotions at the hospital are hard to relive for all of us, even to this day. Sarah was as strong and as classy as ever, obviously shocked and anguished, but dignified in every moment. In her, I saw the iron will and steely composure that my wife inherited. Tom would have been proud of his girls. They exemplified grace in their grief. Nora had told me all the stories of her life with him. Tom wasn't an athlete. His muscular disorder precluded him from engaging in sports, but that didn't stop him from buying gloves and balls and playing catch in the yard with his daughter during her brief foray into softball. Then, when she ventured into cheerleading, he bought every uniform and went to every game, even if he had no rooting interest. His daughter was cheering, so Tom would, too. It didn't matter what Nora did, he was there to support her. If she had decided to become a pool shark, he would have been in every billiard hall in the Midwest while shopping online to have a pool table delivered to his home.

His slight disability had made him accepting, understanding, and generous with others. It also made him persistent and dedicated in everything he did, traits he passed on to his daughter. Nora was a bull terrier when she needed to get something done. Once she sank her teeth in, there was no letting go. But she also was the most understanding and accepting person in the world, in no small part because she had the perfect role model. Tom set a standard for empathy that his daughter followed.

I wish I had been able to communicate those thoughts and feelings to both my wife and my mother-in-law, but, of course, I was no use. Heartbreak and devastation are not emotions you can communicate through sign language. Nora and Sarah were torn to pieces, and I could do little to loosen the straitjacket of grief. In the time I had known him, I had grown to love Tom as a second father, someone I admired and respected. He had raised and shaped the woman who became the love of my life. Nora was suffering, and there was little I could do to help. Not only could I not carry on an adequate, comforting conversation, I couldn't hear the condolences of others. "I just feel so . . ." Nora would say while looking at me before being interrupted by someone else offering their sympathies. Had she completed the sentence? Should I respond? Should I ask her to repeat it? Feel so what?

She had spoken to Tom the day before he died, typical chitchat between a father and his adult daughter. My condition and our plans for the surgery were part of the discussion. She told him she loved him, and he offered the same in reply. There was some comfort in those being the last words they shared. They had also hugged the last time they had been together, at the lunch from which I rushed back to the office to lose my hearing for good. Those two interactions, ordinary and routine, provided some comfort now, and taught me a lesson that I will pass on to anyone who will listen: never take the ordinary encounters of life for granted. Hug often and say "I love you" to your family every day.

We were young to be losing parents—not teenagers or, God forbid, children, but still at a stage when the passing of a loved one hit with more ferocious force. This was a time of weddings, not funerals. My mind went back to a memory from a year or so before. I had been in my office when I got a phone call from a friend I'd grown up with and been close to in high school. We'd remained good enough friends that she knew about my hearing challenges and that I didn't often speak on the phone. There were captioning devices that I used to carry on conversations, but they could be slow and clunky, which led to awkward pauses and inhibited a free-flowing conversation. After I let the call go to voicemail, I looked down and saw that she was calling me again. She knew that I wasn't a phone guy, so I immediately knew that the reason for the outreach couldn't be good.

The second time I answered, and my friend told me that another of our high school friends had died suddenly. We were way too young to be losing classmates. In shock, I said, "What?"

She repeated herself, telling me that our friend had passed away. She thought I meant "What?" as in, "I didn't hear you, what'd you say?" when I was actually expressing shock at the news.

Greeting people as they gathered to memorialize Tom was just as awkward. What's the opening line when these people have come to mourn a friend or relative? "Hi, I'm Matt, Nora's husband, but I can't carry on a conversation with you because I'm deaf, nor can I stand for too long because I might take a spill. But it's nice to meet you, although I wish it were under better circumstances." I would try to speak to Nora, but our discourse had a rhythm that didn't match the setting. She would say something that I missed. In ordinary contexts, when I either asked her to repeat it or guessed and got the answer wrong, she would usually smile and continue to work with me. Sometimes in congested settings, she would say, "Never mind," which was shorthand for "Telling you this in a way you will understand is a lot of work, and it wasn't that important anyway." In this setting, I did my best to minimize the burden by staying out of the way, which was another piece lost from the man I should have been for my family.

The day before the funeral, Nora and I took a walk down the block to the Dairy Queen. As we got close to the restaurant, Nora stopped and raised her eyebrows, her head tilted slightly toward the sky. I let her stand for a minute. When we started walking again, I asked what had happened. She told me that she had heard bagpipes playing "Amazing Grace." At first, I thought it must have been a dream. That sort of serendipity never actually happened. "There's a Catholic church one block over," she said. "They're having a service of some kind."

For the rest of that afternoon and through the funeral the following day, Nora seemed at peace. The pipes had been a wink from Tom, or so she thought. There were more tears, of course, but she sat a little straighter through all the kind words and eulogies offered by Tom's friends and clients. I knew that she needed to process this tragedy, and my situation wasn't helping matters. In less than two months, I would undergo another surgery, with even greater risks than the last time, when I couldn't feel my legs for months. Not only that, but I would be out of work for an extended period, maybe as long as a year. While my employer would welcome me back when I healed, they wouldn't continue to pay me for an extended recovery beyond the company-prescribed sick leave policy. As for so many Americans struggling with health problems, the procedure would cost more than we'd paid for our house, while the recovery from the surgery would cut our income almost in half. Nora was trying to stuff the stages of grief into a box while she dealt with all the other things going on in her life: namely, me.

Nora's newlywed story reads like the Book of Job. What should have been the best time of her life had been one crisis and heartbreak after another. She had known about my condition from our first date, but there is a difference between knowing something is coming in a vague and distant future and facing that reality in the here and now. There is a difference between thinking about your husband someday losing his hearing and suddenly having to communicate everything from "Pass the salt" to "My father just passed away" through a combination of sign language and charades. This was supposed to be the time when couples explored what it meant to be married, making family friends, discussing shared dreams, and talking through where and how we saw ourselves growing old together. Instead, she read peer-reviewed papers on imatinib mesylate, bevacizumab, and aspirin as potential treatments for NF2 while I worked on my balance and tried to adjust to my new soundless world.

Did she have time to grieve? We both hoped so. The whirlwind of everything around us made it difficult to know. There isn't a day that Nora doesn't miss her dad, and there isn't a moment in our lives when I don't wish that I could have done more for her during that awful time.

For many years afterward, Nora would visit that small lake in Indiana on the anniversary of Tom's passing. She always thought about him dying out there alone and cold, so she would go back to talk to him. It took a few years for Nora to tell her mom about the lake trips. They were too personal and, for a while, too painful to share. It was father-daughter time, something she wanted to treasure alone. When she finally mentioned those trips over dinner, her mom smiled from across the table and replied, "I still visit there, too."

At home in the days following the funeral, she continued to work out the insurance and the schedule. We would fly out to California in October for my procedure, where, once again, we would hope for the best.

"Amazing grace, how sweet the sound / That saved a wretch like me."

TEN

A LITTLE LESS CONVERSATION, A LITTLE MORE ACTION,
PLEASE

—Elvis Presley

WE TOOK SARAH WITH US TO LOS ANGELES. She and Nora needed each other, and I needed them both. But before we left, I boned up on the backstory of the scary ride we were all about to board, something I wished I had done before that first surgery that put me in a wheelchair. I'm not much of a history geek—that was always Tom's thing, which he loved to share with us—but the more I learned about the past and the narrative of how we ended up on a plane to the West Coast, the more fascinated I became with the story of enhanced audiology.

I was generally aware of the fact that entire senses could be replaced by science because, like most people, I'd seen it on *Star Trek*. A blind man was able to see with a visor that bypassed his nonworking eyes and stimulated the part of his brain that processes visual input. And despite that challenge, he still managed to rise to be the chief engineer of an entire spaceship. Impressive, for sure. Although in one episode, he was a victim of a brainwashing attempt by the Romulans, who accessed his brain via his implant. At least now I knew to look out for pointy-eared aliens.

It turns out the history of using electrical currents to amplify hearing predates even the USS *Enterprise*. The first known experiment goes all the way back to 1790 and an Italian physicist named Alessandro Volta, the man who invented the electric battery. This discovery was significant enough that the words "volt" and "voltage" come from his name, and he received a bunch of awards from another famous Frenchman named Napoleon. But nine years prior to his breakthrough invention and his proof that electricity could be generated through chemistry, Volta darn near killed himself when he placed two metal rods in his ears and connected them to a circuit, attempting to stimulate greater sound. A college roommate tried something similar our sophomore year, on spring break at a bar in South Padre Island, Texas. The experiment failed for Volta and my friend, leaving both with sizable headaches.

What does this have to do with hearing or music? Really, everything. It was the birth of a pretty fundamental concept in understanding how sound works. Waves enter the ear, vibrating the eardrum and tiny bones, and become electrical impulses that the brain identifies and translates into birds chirping, people talking, and thunder crashing. If, as Volta hypothesized, those impulses could be mimicked or enhanced through an external electrical source, artificial hearing could be created. Back at the South Padre Island bar, my roommate had no hypothesis, he'd just had too many one-dollar Coronas and found a lawn mower battery on the rooftop deck.

The turn of the nineteenth century was a fascinating time for scientists investigating sound, and experiments continued for years thereafter, some rudimentary and others ground-breaking. It was not uncommon in that period for older people to carry around the horns of rams or steers. The old folks would put the small end of the horn in their ears and point the large, open end toward the sound they wanted to hear. While they might not have been able to describe the physics of sound wave compression, they knew that the horn made them hear better.

Few, even among early physicians, understood the complexities of the inner ear. Doctors have known for some time that the malleus, incus, and stapes, which are the smallest bones in the human body, vibrate against something called the cochlea. But what, exactly, happened from there?

It was a question that baffled the smartest doctors in the world from the days of the Roman Empire until the mid-nineteenth century, when scientists began experimenting with a pea-sized organ shaped like a snail's shell that almost no one could figure out. The name "cochlea" comes from the ancient Greek word *kokhlias,* meaning spiral shell, because its shape was really all anyone knew about it for millennia.

Those tiny vibrating bones of the middle ear cause fluid inside the cochlea to ripple, like when you shake the sides of an inflatable kiddy pool. Inside this pool are even tinier hair cells that sway to the music, or, more precisely, move with the ripples. This waving of hair-cell bundles inside the cochlea creates an electric charge, like shuffling your socked feet on the carpet and then touching someone to give them a pop. That electrical charge builds up to stimulate various auditory nerves, which send that electrical signal to the brain.

If that sounds complicated, you should try reading it in a medical journal. I've given you the *Schoolhouse Rock* version. The best way to sum up what happens is that it's as close to a miracle as I've ever seen. When you study the intricacies of the outer, middle, and inner ear and all the steps that have to happen in order for a human to hear a baby cry or a door slam, it's hard not to be awed by the beauty and complexity of the process.

The hair cells at the biggest part of the cochlea pick up the highest-pitched sounds, and as the spiral gets smaller, the hair cells pick up lower and lower tones. Each of those hair-cell clusters picks up and releases ions at an incredible rate of speed and sends signals to the brain even faster—we're talking millions if not billions of transactions every day. That is how hearing people can capture the intricacies of a symphony, the intimidation of a truck horn, and the intimacy of a spouse's snore without thinking about it.

Now you know why doctors specialize in this stuff.

So, imagine the cochlea—which is what people mean when they use the term "inner ear," as in, "he has inner-ear problems"—as an artist. We'll call him "Duke Cochlea," because that's a solid made-up name. Our hero Duke has a palette full of paints in front of him and a blank canvas on which to work. Duke opens the door to his studio that overlooks the most beautiful landscape imaginable, complete with blue sky, puffy white clouds, a rainbow in the distance, trees, mountains, lakes, rocks, a waterfall, and blooming flowers of every conceivable color. If Duke wanted to paint that image onto his canvas using one hand and a brush, it would take months, maybe years, to complete. But Duke doesn't have months or years. He has a nanosecond, a fraction of time that passes so fast the brain can hardly comprehend it. Duke would need thousands of hands and tens of thousands if not hundreds of thousands of different paints, all working in perfect sequence to complete the painting faster than the blink of an eye.

That's what the cochlea does with sound. It's why you instantly catch the echo when you hear John Bonham rip out the opening drum line to "When the Levee Breaks," and why those of you with a taste for classical music can blend every part of Mozart's overture to *The Marriage of Figaro*. Your cochlea takes the vibrations of all those sounds, and just as the ten thousand hands of the artist Duke Cochlea paint a masterpiece in a nanosecond, millions of hair cells send ions to the auditory nerves and you hear every part of one of the most famous tunes in classical music.

If you look at the outer ear—that part you can see while sitting across from someone at a dinner table—you notice that it is shaped like an elaborate funnel, with curves and contours designed to capture and compress sound waves before sending them down the canal. The intensity of those sound waves is what gives noise volume. The frequency is what gives it pitch.

In air, for example, sound travels at eleven hundred feet per second. That's why outdoorsmen will count the seconds between seeing a flash of lightning and hearing the clap of thunder. Divide that time by five and you know how many miles away the strike occurred. But you can also get a good sense of how close you are by the volume of the boom. The closer you are to a source of noise, the tighter the wave and the louder the sound.

People with good hearing can also pick up a difference in sound frequency of less than 0.5 percent. That's why a record producer can tell if a vocalist is off pitch by a fraction of a degree, and it is why someone like Arthur Fiedler, the famed conductor of the Boston Pops Orchestra, could likely tell if a single oboist was playing with a toothache.

This was all fascinating, some of which I had read about in school—but the medical side always seemed just out of reach for my marketing-centered brain. In fact, when a resident once made reference to my hearing leaving me, I tuned out the medical jargon that immediately followed. Those words, "leaving me," suggest this was maybe just a trial separation, one where my hearing might come back after a few nights to think about things at a Courtyard Marriott. John Denver's voice has a way of making me feel like problems are never as bad as they seem, that everything will be okay. Instead of listening to the resident explain whatever it was I needed to know, my brain had retreated to Denver singing, *"Leaving on a jet plane, / Don't know when I'll be back again. / Oh, babe, I hate to go."*

While the science stuff didn't stick with me, the stories of how we got where we are, how one generation stood on the shoulders of the previous one to create the miracles of modern auditory technology, captured my interest. What drove these people to do what they did? What inspiration did they find?

In the 1950s, a French scientist named André Djourno developed a device that remotely stimulated motor nerves, hoping to make the paralyzed walk. Then, in 1957, another French scientist named Charles Eyriès implanted Djourno's device in a deaf human test subject and successfully stimulated the auditory nerve. The deaf subject heard an awful racket, but he did hear, which was the point of the experiment.

Building on the work of Djourno and Eyriès, the first cochlear impact was put into a patient's inner ear in 1961 in Los Angeles by doctors William House and John Doyle. These were California scientists who had spent years working on improving hearing among the profoundly deaf. Their breakthrough was followed three years later by a team from Stanford University who placed a six-channel electrode directly into the cochlea of a subject. With success in both of those experiments, another team, at UC San Francisco, began clinical trials in the early 1970s, and in 1973, the first international conference on the "electrical stimulation of the acoustic nerve as a treatment for sensorineural deafness in man" took place in San Francisco. Four years later, in 1977, the first peer-reviewed evaluation of patients with what we now know as cochlear impacts was published.

The world of the hearing impaired changed forever at that point. External, electronic stimulation of auditory nerves worked. The deaf could hear. Not everything. Not perfectly. But they could hear something. *Star Trek* was right. Drs. House and Doyle had created something that could restore one of the five senses, a revolution on par with Alexander Graham Bell inventing the telephone, or Thomas Edison's lightbulb.

The reason more people have never heard of House and Doyle is because not that many people are totally deaf. Bell's and Edison's inventions changed everyone's lives. House and Doyle's invention changed the lives of those who couldn't hear. It's still a big deal, one worth knowing and celebrating, but not one that would make the cover of *Time* magazine.

In 1984, the cochlear implant was given the seal of approval by the FDA, and in the decades since, advancements in the quality of the sound and speech processors have been the stuff of science fiction. The internet is full of videos of people hearing for the first time, from babies hearing their mother's voices to adults hearing the technician who turned on the device, followed by their own gasping sobs. The first and most famous viral video was from 2011, when a twenty-nine-year-old woman named Sarah Churman had her implant turned on and heard the technician say, "Okay, so now technically, the device is on." After a moment of laughter, Churman burst into tears of joy. Eleven million views later, she was featured on network morning shows and was a guest of Ellen DeGeneres. Those stories are touching and inspiring, worth an hour of your time and a box or two of tissues.

But they are not my story, and not the story of NF2.

I like to describe the difference between someone with a functioning cochlea and normal auditory nerves and someone who suffers from neurofibromatosis type 2 with another art analogy, one that is a little more rudimentary. Remember that rich kid in first grade who came to school with the giant box of Crayola crayons, all sixty-four colors, with names like burnt sienna and sky blue? Someone always ironed that kid's khakis and turned up his collar as if he was about to sail in the America's Cup. But the box of crayons was perfect, a full panoply of everything you could want—mountain meadow, cadet blue, atomic tangerine, neon carrot—the box even had a built-in sharpener. That kid with his crayons is a person with normal hearing.

Those of us with NF2 who get an implant have the three-pack of crayons you get with the kids' menu at Applebee's.

Don't get me wrong, we are lucky to have the three colors, even if two of them are black and gray. Dr. William F. House of the House Ear Institute in Los Angeles, who implanted the first cochlear device into a patient, realized not long after his invention was approved by the FDA that it did not help people who had no auditory nerves, or people like me who suffered from NF2. Not content to let a segment of the deaf population go untreated, House and his colleagues began work to bypass the cochlea and stimulate the auditory nerves directly in the brainstem.

On May 24, 1979, House and another doctor named William Hitselberger placed the first auditory brainstem implant (ABI) into a fifty-one-year-old woman who had lost all her hearing due to tumors on her auditory nerves. That device had a single electrode attached next to the cochlea nucleus, which provided the patient with sound awareness but not much else. In other words, she could hear noise, but could not distinguish between Bach and a bullhorn. Still, she wore the ABI for the rest of her life.

The difference between the cochlear implant (CI) and the ABI is that the CI stimulates the nerves in the cochlea, those that are already designed to distinguish sounds. That's why a forty-year-old woman in England who has been deaf her entire life can have a CI implanted and immediately hear her technician recite the days of the week and months of the year, and why she can understand her husband when he asks, "Can you hear me?" The cochlea is still doing some of the work, but it has been enhanced by surgically implanted electrodes.

The ABI bypasses the first part of that process and goes straight to the brain. House and his team could stimulate the nerves, but they couldn't refine them. So, while sound could be created by going straight to the brain, it was like turning on the amplifiers at a Kiss concert and then handing the instruments to kindergartners.

More patients had ABIs installed in the early and mid-eighties. In 1987, the first paper was published showing that patients with ABIs experienced tone perception and significant auditory discrimination. They could tell that sounds were different and tell where they were originating, but there was a lot of work to be done.

Still, with the advancements in cochlear implants and ABIs since the 1980s, total deafness has, for all practical purposes, been "cured." The quotation marks are intentional, because this is where the cultures clash, and our story takes an unexpected twist.

* * *

t is estimated that a million Americans are functionally deaf, but no one knows the actual number. Older people who are losing their hearing slip into the "functionally deaf" category, and then, through the magic of hearing aids, they can carry on a conversation and sing a hymn in a church. There is also an entire hearing loss related culture that communicates using sign language. American Sign Language, which is universally accepted and is what you see being signed whenever a politician gives a speech or a televangelist asks for money, is believed to have originated at the American School for the Deaf in Hartford, Connecticut, in about 1817, although various signing languages were chronicled as far back as the 1500s. Despite being its own unique language common to the hearing loss community, no one has ever known how many people use American Sign Language at any given time. The closest figures came from a census in 1972, which estimated the number at five hundred thousand.

At one point in the not-too-distant past, every state had at least one school for the deaf, a publicly funded institution where the hearing impaired could get an education while also communicating with others in a world of signing. These schools were a godsend. Not only did they allow children to learn and engage with the world without stigma or judgment, but those children could thrive and adapt, developing techniques and methods that allowed them to grow into professional adults in a mostly hearing world.

Not many of those schools exist anymore. In addition to the technology that has allowed the deaf to join the world of sound, schools have mainstreamed the hearing impaired, putting them into the regular school systems.

But there are still a substantial number of people who do not want to be "cured," because as far as they are concerned, there isn't anything "wrong" with not being able to hear. Deafness to the Deaf community is who they are as people. That is why the *D* is capitalized when people write about and discuss the Deaf community and Deaf culture. Losing your hearing is small-d deaf. Embracing your hearing loss and choosing not to change it is big-D Deaf. Those in that community would prefer not to join the hearing world, because they feel as though it robs them of an identity. To those individuals, hearing people are proselytizing a cure for a disease that doesn't exist. Bringing up the implants and other technologies makes people in Deaf culture feel like damaged goods, which is almost never the intention of the person bringing them up but is often the way the conversation is received.

I get it. Both sides of this debate have valid points that they make with great passion. It would be wonderful if both sides would be sensitive to the feelings of the other. Adults within the Deaf community are happy with their lives. They are people of free will and open choices. Deaf culture around the world is worth acknowledging and respecting, no matter what you choose.

For me, the choice was easy. I had been told about ABIs not long after my first surgery, the one that put me in a wheelchair for a month. A neurologist had given me the lowdown: the ABI was still in the buggy-whip stage. Where CIs are common, ABIs are rare, in part because they are newer, but also because the condition that requires them is as uncommon as you can get. Only about one in forty thousand people have NF2, and many of them go undiagnosed until it is too late. The average age when NF2 affects a person is between eighteen and twenty-four, a time when most people feel healthy and invincible. The last thing they do is go the doctor when their hearing gets hazy. By the time they are diagnosed, the tumors are creating a lot more problems than just hearing loss. But from a technology perspective, since it's a small universe of patients that need ABIs, the advancements have come at a slower pace.

I describe hearing aids as being like painted lines on the highway, a wonderful guide to help get you where you're going. A CI is like putting up incandescent streetlights, a significant improvement in terms of moving you along. But neither of those things matter if the bridge is out. An ABI is a detour around the broken bridge. The implant zips right past the ear canal and cochlea and directly to the brainstem.

Sadly, it turns out *Star Trek* isn't a documentary and humans were not designed to have electrodes attached to their brains. The brainstem is only a couple of centimeters in diameter, but billions of impulses run back and forth through it every second, telling your body to do everything from pumping blood in and out of the chambers of your heart, to blinking when your eyes get dry, to grabbing a fork when dinner arrives. When you surgically implant a device that looks like a tiny flyswatter into the stem, your brain says, "What is the world is that? That's not how this works."

The brain, of course, is right. Surgeons are not sure exactly how it works, either. They are good at what they do, but they admit to having limited knowledge about what goes on where inside the brain. They think they know what section of the brainstem controls hearing, but they could just as easily be implanting a device that makes your leg shake all the time. The best case, as it was described to me, would be for the surgeons to hit the mark with the electrodes, and I still might not be able to hear.

As far as tamping down expectations, my guys did a great job. They told me not to expect anything life altering. They suggested that I ignore all those heartwarming videos of people hearing "I love you" for the first time. I might hear something called "life noises," where you recognize a ruckus but have no idea if it's a car alarm or your wife saying, "I'm home." Everything, I was warned, could sound like a gravel truck.

I asked for some contacts, maybe people who had gone through this, a support group of sorts who could talk to me about their experiences. This was years before social media outlets like Facebook created platforms for everything and everyone, and then, as now, doctors and hospitals couldn't just hand out the numbers or email addresses of patients. That lack of community made me feel as though I were in a universe of one, isolated and alone. Finally, one of the administrators at the House Institute found another NF2 patient who had gotten an ABI and was willing to communicate with me. For the next few days, I emailed back and forth with a man in Alabama whom I'd never met, but with whom I shared an inexorable bond. We chatted at length about our histories, our surgeries, our experiences going deaf, and our anxieties about what life would be like in the future.

Finally, I asked him about his ABI surgery and how the implant was working out for him. While I'm not sure what I expected, the words "It was awful. Don't do it" did not register at first. My mind immediately went back to high school and the lunch I'd had with the cadet from West Point who told me not to seek an appointment. Then, as now, the response hit me between the eyes. Since this was email and not a text chat with modern shorthand and a thousand emojis, I listed several questions to get a better understanding of what he had experienced and what I could expect. He answered them all, but the crux of the response was simple: there were now a dozen electrodes in his brainstem and a magnet in his skull, and when he turned the thing on, all he heard was the roar of a tractor engine with a screeching fan belt.

Having been through one brain surgery already, I knew that it could be a crapshoot. The surgeon might think he had attached an electrode to one of the audio sensors in your brainstem when actually he got the nerve that makes your pinky finger twitch, but the process had gotten better with each try. They don't call it "practicing medicine" for nothing. Like anything, the more you practice, the better you get. I felt certain that my email pal in Alabama was a case of one bad outcome, an outlier whom doctors used as a case study to learn and improve. Always the optimist, I knew that my situation would be different.

I also was convinced that this was the right thing. One of the best traits I inherited from my father was pragmatism. If you need something done, you do it. Vanity is not part of the equation. That was the case when I needed glasses in school, and it was the case when I needed brain surgery and discs attached to my head in order to hear. If it solved a problem, or moved us closer to a solution, I didn't hesitate.

Deep down, I desperately wanted this to work. I realized that learning sign language was like learning Mandarin. It's fun to throw out a few phrases at the local Chinese restaurant, but unless you are immersed in it and have someone with whom to communicate every day, you are never going to be fluent. I wanted to hear something. The good part about losing your hearing slowly is that you adapt and compromise for so long that you forget there ever was a perfect. But total silence was not my life. If there was a medical way to make this happen, I was all for it.

Nora scheduled the surgery. The House Institute in Los Angeles is still one of the only places doing ABI implantation. By this time I was an old pro with hospital visits, although each one carried a new set of anxieties. When your last one left you in a wheelchair and a rehab facility, you enter with a jaundiced eye. Southern California is year-round beautiful. Once inside the hospital, though, we could have been in Kalamazoo. Once you get past the beautiful eggshell floors, walls, and ceilings (everything in the place seemed to be one shade or another of white), there isn't a lot different in any hospital. The IV needles are all individually sealed, and there are the same curtains set on rollers in tracks in the ceiling so they can be easily pulled aside if a lot of medical staff need to rush to a bed at once. Heart monitors don't change much from spot to spot, and neither do the scrubs the nurses wear when they shave and prod and go through all the procedures that precede surgery.

This was the first procedure I had where I was functionally deaf, which made communicating with the nurses interesting. They always have a litany of things to go over, some mundane, like the fact that you need to take off any jewelry, including your wedding ring, before being wheeled away, and some jarring, like the acknowledgment that any step in this process could conceivably kill you. The tumors would need to be removed again before the implant was installed. Those darn things were still growing, and we had to dig into the Pringles can again to get them out, hopefully with fewer side effects this time around. The tumors had finally accomplished their devious mission and robbed me of all my hearing. But they would continue to grow, and I would continue to need to have them surgically removed, with the same set of risks each time. No matter how good doctors get at this, brain surgery will never be like getting your appendix removed. Even the best ballplayer in the world strikes out a few times.

All hospitals have a peculiar, antiseptic smell, as if someone has tried to mask the burning odor of an ammonia-based cleaning chemical with a thousand truck-stop air fresheners. The beeps and the charts and the computer screens are all the same as well. There's a whiteboard in every room identifying a "nurse on duty," among other things. The nurses tend to give you a little warning before pulling back the curtain and barging into your temporary personal space. Doctors show no such decorum. They zip back the curtain and start talking before looking you in the eye. Again, that's a problem when you are deaf, although the folks at the House Institute were accustomed and prepared for all levels of hearing impairment. NF2 might be rare in the general population, but the folks at House saw it every day.

A team of doctors paraded through to say hi and explain their role in the upcoming performance. A chipper anesthesiologist asked about allergies and if I'd ever had any adverse reaction to being sedated. As tempting as it was, I didn't say, "Other than not being able to walk, stand, or feel my legs for a couple of months after waking up the last time?" I love to joke about everything, but good comedy is about timing, and with Nora in the room, this wasn't the right time. I did say something like, "Hopefully I'll hear you afterward," which was lame, even by my sad-joke standards. At this point, since I couldn't hear anyway, I was ready to break into my best Elvis impersonation: *"A little less conversation, a little more action, please / All this aggravation ain't satisfactioning me."*

I can only imagine how that would have gone over.

Soon came a bald, bespectacled guy with a wry grin and a Marcus Welby manner named Derald Brackmann. He was the star of the show. In addition to devoting his entire career to otology and neurotology, he was the world's leading expert on NF2 and auditory brainstem implants. If there was anyone you wanted in the room while you were in the midst of brain surgery, this was the guy.

What I didn't know at the time was that Dr. Brackmann had another claim to fame. He and Dr. House were the developers of the House-Brackmann Scale for facial paralysis, a uniform grading scale to measure the severity of nerve damage when a person has a paralyzed face. It's a six-grade scale. Grade one is normal. You can move every muscle in your face, blink your eyes, raise your eyebrows to show off some forehead wrinkles, smile, wink, crinkle your nose, purse your lips, and feel your cheeks when you pinch them: all the things you take for granted.

Grade two is slight facial weakness. Your eye closes on its own unless you work to keep it open, and the mouth is asymmetrical when you use it or when you engage the other muscles in your face.

Grade three is a little more severe but still unnoticeable at rest, except for the eyes, which will close unless you force them open, and the mouth, which goes catawampus at a moment's notice.

Grade four is when things get serious. The eyes won't close all the way, and blinking becomes a problem, which means the tear ducts don't work properly. Cheek and forehead movement is limited, and there are obvious problems with the mouth.

Grade five is when you lose your ability to smile, or close your eyes, or move your forehead. You don't feel anything in your face when you touch it.

And grade six is full facial paralysis.

Why, you may ask, did a couple of doctors working on auditory brainstem implants come up with a facial paralysis chart?

That's a question whose answer I learned the hard way.

On October 6, 2004, I went in to have an ABI implanted and a couple of additional tumors removed. The last thing

I remember when I was wheeled into the operating theater was a sense of cold and the thought that they really should make those hospital gowns a little thicker. The anesthesiologist leaned in so that I could see him and signaled with a thumbs-up that I was about to go to sleep.

When I woke up again, half my face was paralyzed, and again I couldn't walk. Within a couple of minutes, my eyes dried out because I couldn't blink. The average person blinks about fifteen to twenty times a minute, not only to moisturize the eyes but to clean them. Eyelids are both the windshield washer and wiper of your eyeballs. All of a sudden, mine didn't work; I had to have drops added constantly. Then, when I tried to drink water, which my body was screaming for after the surgery, liquid poured down the side of my jaw and onto my chest. Now, I couldn't even eat or drink properly. Was I back to using a sippy cup?

Three years after my first surgery, which left me wondering if I would ever walk again, I was in the same boat with a dastardly new crew of gremlins. I also had double vision. And I was still deaf.

I knew things could go sideways—there were always risks—but this was worse than I had expected.

The long and winding road continued. Where it would lead us remained an open question.

ELEVEN

THIS VOICE KEEPS WHISPERING IN MY OTHER EAR

TELLS ME I MAY NEVER SEE YOU AGAIN.

—The Eagles

WE HAD BEEN TOLD THAT I HAD A 1 PERCENT CHANCE OF SOME FACIAL NERVE DAMAGE BECAUSE OF THE LOCATION AND SIZE OF THE TUMOR. You don't spend a lot of time worrying about the 1 percent risks in life. If you did, you'd never go into the ocean again after watching Shark Week and you sure wouldn't go outside in a thunderstorm. For that reason, something between surprise and "you have got to be kidding me" shock swept over me when I woke up and couldn't feel or move the left side of my face. We were told that the tumor had not only overwhelmed my hearing nerve, but it had also elbowed its way onto my facial and vestibular nerves, the latter of which controls balance. Turns out those are all crammed close together. When a tumor grows on one, there's a chance it can affect the others. My balance had been off for a while, which is not uncommon with someone experiencing hearing loss. The difference is that most people lose their balance because of trouble in the middle ear, not because of a brain tumor.

To say the facial paralysis was a disappointment undersold the situation. It was awful. For starters, even people with perfect hearing communicate through facial expressions and movement. When approached by a stranger on the street, before the first utterance you size up whether their intentions are hostile or friendly by looking at their face. Is he menacing? Is he about to ask directions? Does he think he knows you and is about to embarrass himself by saying hello? Is he about to return something you dropped half a block back? The face gives you a sense of where the interaction is going before the first word is spoken. Sincerity, self-assurance, honesty, generosity: we evaluate those things through nonverbal cues.

The thought of losing that sent me into a mild panic. When I first looked in the mirror, the asymmetrical face staring back at me caused my heart to leap. On the right side, I could see my cheeks tighten and the tiny muscles in the corner of my eye contract, an unconscious reflex response to shock or fear. I raised my right eyebrow and drew back half of my mouth in an astonished gasp. The other half drooped like the jowls of a sleeping hound dog. Half my forehead didn't move, and my eye looked artificial, like something animatronic in a Disney ride.

Shock gave way to sadness, bordering on depression. For the vast majority of my life, I had naturally compensated for hearing loss by being the most expressive person in any interaction. I could stare at you with an aggressive interest in what you were saying, because that provided my only mechanism for following along. I needed to engage people through the way I looked. A nod and a smile meant "I got it." A slight tilt of the head and a curious furrowing of the brow meant "I didn't catch that." Opening the eyes wide and leaning in meant "Oh, wow, that's amazing."

Not that vanity should have played a role in my feelings at that moment, but as a lover of Discovery Channel, I had learned that a leading criterion in the animal kingdom for finding a mate was physical symmetry. My facial paralysis meant I wasn't just being vain; I was scientifically proven to be less attractive. Look at the scariest masks. None of them line up correctly. Think of the *Scream* mask or the off-kilter hockey mask worn by Jason Voorhees in the *Friday the 13th* movies. People instinctively pause when confronted with an asymmetrical face, especially on a young person who you would assume has not suffered a stroke.

Communication is a two-way street, and I spent years preparing myself for a world of one-way streets due to my inability to receive information. But now, with no time to prepare at all, I opened my eyes in the ICU to streets that were closed for repairs indefinitely, all because I could no longer effectively convey information. Plus, I looked like hell.

I also felt as though I had been robbed of my most potent weapon: my ability to find humor in almost all things. I had always used a joke and a smile as a coping mechanism. There wasn't a deaf joke I wouldn't tell or a one-liner I wouldn't throw out. The key to those landing the right way was my expression. Did I say that weirdly dark thing with a twinkle in my eye and the hint of a grin on my face, or was I really demented? Without the benefit of half my face, the answer wasn't obvious.

On Drs. House and Brackmann's scale, the left side of my face was a solid six, specifically *VI*. Something about the roman numerals made it feel gothic and worse.

Six—*VI*
ORAL—No Movement
MIDFACE—No Movement
EYE—No Movement
BROW—No Movement

I couldn't move anything on the left side, including my mouth or eye. To her credit, Nora didn't recoil in horror, or even look concerned. Even through her still-fresh grief after the loss of her father, she immediately smiled and stroked the part of my hair peeking out from under the bandages as if everything had gone fine. I was alive, after all, which is not a foregone conclusion anytime someone pokes round in your brain to remove a tumor. The surgeons told us that they had done their best to reconnect the facial nerve, but the procedure had been like trying to connect two pieces of dental floss while riding a train through the Alps. The good news was, we would know if any of what they'd done with those flossy nerve endings had worked . . . within a year.

As déjà vu goes, the "we'll know where we are in a year" moment wasn't one I had hoped to relive. I needed the incisions to heal and scar tissue to harden before we could turn on the implant to see if it worked, so my hearing, which was nonexistent, would remain that way for at least a few more months.

But I had a more pressing problem. I couldn't close my left eye. Blinking is not just for cleaning your eye, it's also a moisturizing mechanism. Without the involuntary batting of the eyelids, the eyes can't lubricate. Blinking replenishes the tear film, which is a thin, outer layer of water on the cornea. And without the tear film, you can't see. That moisture provides a smooth surface for light to pass through. It also helps move oxygen to the cornea, which is vital to sight because the cornea has no blood vessels. It relies on the tear film for oxygen. That's why dry eyes hurt. Your eyes are telling your brain to get them some air. This is a detailed and medical way of saying we all take our flimsy little eyelids for granted.

For a brief time I felt like Malcolm McDowell in *A Clockwork Orange*, unblinking, with drops being applied nonstop so that I didn't lose my eye. The options I was given were both clear and lousy.

1. Have drops applied every few minutes for the rest of my life and then tape my eye closed every night. This sounded like an enormous inconvenience.

2. Have my eyelid sewn shut. This option sounded medieval.

3. Have a tiny spring hinge that looked like a mangled paper clip surgically installed in my eyelid to assist with closure.

The clock was ticking, which meant we didn't have the opportunity to do much research or talk through the pros and cons. Nora and I are planners who try our best to see things coming. We always want to prepare. Ironically, we hadn't contemplated the eye thing. This trip was supposed to be about hearing. My eye was visibly red and irritated and only getting worse, so we'd need to make a decision right away.

Of course, vision is important to everyone, but I think I can selfishly claim that for me, a guy who lost all his hearing just a few months prior, my vision was vital. When you can't hear, sight becomes a primary means of communication. Without lipreading or at least the ability to sign, I would be cut off from everything and everyone. It was hard enough having Nora translate for me. If I couldn't make eye contact with a person speaking and then turn to her and either see her mouth or watch her hands, my world would shrink to only those things that were an arm's length away. I spoke with Nora for about a minute before we decided. It had only been two days and I'd already applied eye drops more than two hundred times. That wasn't sustainable for another sixty years.

Option 1 was out. And I wasn't ready to go full pirate, so Option 2 was off the table. We went with option 3. We entrusted one of my remaining senses to the mangled paper clip.

With more time, we might have learned that this procedure was being performed by a plastic surgeon in Beverly Hills who had pioneered it, and that said procedure did not have Food and Drug Administration approval. I probably would have asked a thousand questions. Prior to my ABI surgery, we had been cooped up in an extended-stay hotel across the street from the House Institute, where we had gone over every question, every potential side effect (like the 1 percent chance my face would be paralyzed), and every good and bad outcome of the procedure. Now, just out of brain surgery, deaf, partially paralyzed, unable to stand without assistance, and with my eye turning redder than the traffic lights on Wilshire Boulevard, Nora and I loaded up in a cab and took the twenty-minute ride through Brentwood and past Century City. Hey, did you know that the Nakatomi Plaza from *Die Hard* is actually the 20th Century Fox building next to the Beverly Hilton Hotel? It might have been nice to get out and take some pictures if I hadn't been a couple of days post-op from brain surgery and on my way to an emergency eye procedure.

The doctor's office looked like a place where you would get a new prescription for bifocals. After we waited seven agonizing hours, a doctor finally came out and gave us the lowdown. The eyelid spring, as we were told, isn't a coil like you'd find in a fountain pen. It is a wire loop with two arms and looks like a door hinge or a miniature version of the compass you used in middle school geometry. The wire loop is placed under the skin near the bridge of your nose with one wire extending under your eyebrow. The other is placed into the eyelid itself. Gold weights are often added to the lid to provide a balance between closed and open. The effect is like one of those creepy dolls from the 1970s with eyes that open when upright and close when lying down.

We scheduled the procedure for the following morning, and I spent the next twelve hours dousing my eyeball with artificial tears.

The theme for the week seemed to be "let's leave Matt some surprises." A big one came when I was told that the surgery required me to be awake. I had just come out of one of the most complex and groundbreaking surgeries in human history, with an electrode now implanted in my brainstem, and I didn't remember a second of it because when the anesthesiologist asked me to count backward from ten, I didn't make it to nine. But for an eyelid-spring implant, the patient is an active participant. If the spring was too loose, my eye wouldn't close. If it was too tight, the eye wouldn't open. I had to be awake to follow the surgeon's instructions on opening and closing.

Early that morning, in yet another hospital, I lay awake on a gurney in the basement hallway with a lot of other patients lined up like zombies, since they were all asleep. I had no phone to play with, no clock to count the minutes, no sound to connect to my environment: even the stained ceiling tiles were a blur due to my ever-dehydrated eyeball. My only thought was: this would be a great opening scene in a horror movie.

Then, before I could complete my thought, scrubbed-up surgical teams came to roll each of my zombie friends into a different room. When it was finally my turn to be rolled away, the nurse didn't look at me or say a word. Not that I would have heard her, but it would have been nice to see her lips move and get some sense that a conversation had been attempted. They were obviously accustomed to sedated patients. At that moment, I'd have given her a car for a pat on my arm and one of those smiles that says, "I know you're scared, but we're going to take great care of you." Instead, my rolling bed just hit a wall on the way through the automatic doors.

About eight nurses prepped the room with military precision—instruments here, monitors there. I was covered in paper everywhere except my eyes, so I could see the surgical tools that would be cutting into my flesh a fraction of an inch from my eyeball. With that thought in mind, I looked to see if the little peaks on the heart monitor registered the palpitations I felt.

One week over the summer in high school, I traveled with a Methodist youth group to work at a children's camp in the Appalachian Mountains. Among many wonderful experiences that week, it was where I learned that AM radio waves bounce, making them easier to hear in remote mountains. One evening, our group sat around after a Sam's Club frozen lasagna dinner and tuned into an AM classic rock station. That's when I first heard Burton Cummings of The Guess Who sing *"These eyes are cryin' / These eyes have seen a lot of loves / But they're never gonna see another one like I had with you."*

In that operating room, this line, one from a song I hadn't thought about in years, kept running through my head. A Midwestern kid, out West, recalling a Canadian band he'd heard on a Southern trip, singing about crying eyes before undergoing surgery because his eyes won't cry. Yeah, I think "surreal" is a fair word to describe the moment.

Soon blue scrubs were replaced by white scrubs as the surgeon proceeded to treat me like a body being autopsied. Our only interaction during the ordeal was when he would hold his closed fist over my field of vision to tell me to try to close my eye, followed by an open hand when he wanted me to open the eyelid.

I watched as the scalpel went straight for my eye, held by someone I knew nothing about and had met only once the day before. I'd been given some numbing drops, not that it mattered since I still couldn't feel anything other than my quickening breath and racing heart. This had to be act II of the zombie movie, right?

I felt pressure as the scalpel went into my eyelid. That's when my vision blurred. I could only see shadows. For a moment, I thought the surgeon had cut into my cornea and that I was permanently blind. Then I felt and tasted blood as it ran down the side of my face and into the corner of my mouth.

I probably should have been alarmed, but instead I was relieved. I wasn't blind; I was just bleeding profusely and awake on an operating table.

A nurse hustled in to clean up the gore, and I could see again, just in time to catch a glimpse of the eyelid spring. Up close, as in about a millimeter from my eye, that twisted paper clip someone had been playing with when a meeting went too long was now inside my eyelid.

Just a couple of days before, I'd been sharing a cookies-and-cream milkshake with my beautiful newlywed bride (one shake, two straws. Ah, young love) in a good part of Los Angeles, not far from the Playboy Mansion and below the hills where Jackson Browne wrote songs with titles like "Doctor My Eyes" and "Here Come Those Tears Again." I'd come here because I couldn't hear. Now, I was on an operating table, awake under lamps that could light Fenway, watching a guy I didn't know handle a scalpel around my eye to insert a steel contraption that looked like it had been run over by a Prius. Another California band described this moment to perfection. *"Sometimes the light's all shining on me / Other times I can barely see."*

The Grateful Dead wasn't a band I knew as well, but my "coolest" high school friend, Anna Beth, loved them and that was enough for me. I was making a case to my parents to allow me to road trip to Indianapolis to camp out and see them at Deer Creek (man, music venues had great names before sponsorships became a thing) in the weeks after high school graduation with a friend. We didn't have tickets but felt sure we'd figure it out, whatever that meant. Besides, it felt like a very Grateful Dead concertgoer experience to not have any plan. Anna Beth wouldn't have had one. The timing was perfect because they were performing over the Fourth of July weekend—we'd go up Monday for the show and come back Tuesday. Mom didn't like anything about the idea but never said "no." Her decision ended up being made for her when concertgoers crashed the fence at Sunday night's show, causing the band to cancel Monday's performance. Five weeks later, Jerry had a fatal heart attack near his home in Northern California. For a band I regretfully never got to hear live, I'm not sure there's a single line in music that resonated more with me as I laid awake in that operating room than *"Lately it occurs to me / What a long strange trip it's been."*

With the device inserted, what looked like a giant fish-hook entered my field of vision. These were the stitches being stitched, swirling and looping and pressing hard against my eye. I didn't feel the needle pricks, but I felt the pressure. It was as if my eyeball was being pushed into the back of my skull.

Then a bloody-gloved hand entered my view with a thumbs-up. It was over. I would be wheeled out to recovery, or so I thought. Instead, I continued to lie in the operating theater as the nurses cleaned up. The carnage on the sheets and paper made me tighten my grip on the table. How was this even possible? I like CSI shows, and I imagine them entering the room as a crime scene and seeing this mess. "Look at all of that, we're going to need a team in here to get this cleaned up as soon as we're done."

"Do we know what we're dealing with here?"

"An eyelid, sir."

Finally, I was wheeled back out into the basement hallway, where I waited a few minutes before being pushed into recovery. I'm sure the whole thing would have hurt if I could have felt anything.

When Nora came in, I saw her gasp and then quickly try to disguise it as something else. Oh, boy, that can't be good. Just a day ago, she had seen me with the face of an evil ventriloquist dummy and offered nothing but smiles and a kiss on the head. Now, she appeared aghast.

Between the stitches and the swelling, I looked like I'd been in a fistfight with Ivan Drago that nobody stopped after

I went down. Realizing she had just shown her shocked face, she shifted to sympathy, which, in my view, wasn't much better. That look turned to impatience tinged with anger when the doctor came in to give his postgame speech. My new look, combined with paralysis and staples from brain surgery, gave off a real *Batman*-villain vibe. That was not the look we were going for, and certainly not what my former med-school student and medical-sales-representative wife expected.

Undeterred, the surgeon said everything had gone well, and my follow-up treatment should be ice and heat, alternating, to bring the swelling down. Then he vanished. We were sent on our way, Beauty and the Beast, two thousand miles from home.

The eye problem compounded the balance issues. Your vestibular nerve is what allows you to walk around in the dark or stand on one foot with your eyes closed. Because mine was damaged by the tumor, I had to rely on eyesight to keep my balance, and even then, I might tumble over at any moment. Walking would require a cane for the foreseeable future, and driving was out of the question.

Most people don't think about all the problems that come with losing feeling and movement in half your face, because those who experience it are usually having a stroke, which means there are far more pressing concerns. For example, how do you know when you bite your cheek or tongue when you can't feel either? The answer is, you don't until you look down and see blood on your shirt.

The second problem is how to chew and swallow food.

When half your mouth doesn't work, you risk choking on anything more solid than chicken soup. Gum is out of the question, and something as simple as an almond M&M, the greatest food product ever conceived by man, presented a choking hazard unless it was pulverized before going into my mouth.

There was another wrinkle. Because I had a foreign device in my brainstem, doctors warned me not to lift anything heavier than a cup of coffee. No taking a couple of trash bags outside or pushing the can to the curb. No moving items around in the house or helping get groceries from the back of the car. And no lifting a suitcase, which meant that Nora and her mother were my valets at LAX as we headed home. It was impossible to miss the stares. Strangers looked at me and shuddered reflexively before looking away. Kids pointed before their parents shushed them and pushed their hands down. It's a feeling you would never wish on anyone, even though, had I been on the other end, I am ashamed to think I would have done the same. I wanted to stand on a chair and say, "It's not what you think. I wasn't mugged or in some horrible nuclear accident. I didn't escape from a circus. Some of this was actually elective. I chose . . . this. Anyway, my wife and mother-in-law are doing the whole luggage thing because I just had brain surgery and anything that would contract the muscles in the head and neck, which lifting anything more than a pound or so would, is off-limits. And, oh, by the way, my father-in-law, her husband [pointing at Sarah] and her father [pointing at Nora], recently passed away in a tragic accident."

Everyone with the airline was kind and chipper, just like everyone had been at the House Institute. I guess it was hard not be upbeat in Southern California, but I could have used some company in my misery. Nora was the strong one, a beautiful, brilliant, and confident woman with her stumbling, deaf, partially paralyzed, one-eyed husband, who had been instructed to keep ice on his eye for the first twenty-four hours after surgery. That was hard during the flight, as I couldn't lie down and didn't have much elbow room. So I created a harness over my head with a pouch that I filled with airplane ice cubes, which I realized are the fastest melting ice on the planet. Somewhere over Nevada I felt water run down the front of my shirt and into my seat to mix with the crumbs of the pureed food that had fallen out of my drooping mouth. Insult to injury, indeed.

It would be three months before I could have my device turned on, the last piece of the ABI process. We'd come back and I'd get the disc that people could see. The flyswatter-shaped electrode array was in my brainstem, with a wire running to a magnet and receptor in my skull, under the skin above and slightly behind my ear. The last part was the battery-powered receiver. Pop it onto the magnet and, in theory, sound would be captured and transferred directly to my brain.

In the meantime, I had some therapies to work out. I had gotten a little better at sign language out of necessity. Nora's lips I could read, but there were always things I missed. Did you say, don't eat cat? Thanks for the advice, but the thought never occurred to me. What's that? Oh, "that," not "cat." Don't eat that. Well, that makes a lot more sense.

We worked out a shorthand where she would sign the first letter of the word that might be misunderstood. Some things needed no translation, though. Our first full day back home, she came in and stared at my face with a look of panic. "What happened?" was pretty easy to understand.

"Nothing," I said. "I've been doing what the doctor said and treating my eye with ice and heat."

Nora pointed to the mirror, which I had avoided because, once I was stationary, walking anywhere might lead to a fall. With a cane in one hand and Nora on the other arm, I shuffled to the mirror in the bedroom and realized I had just compounded a complex problem even further. It turns out that alternating heat and ice works fine for bringing swelling down as long as you can feel the area being treated. When you can't, you end up burning your skin with a heating pad that is too hot, and then you freeze your face by keeping the ice on too long, which does the opposite of promoting blood flow.

It didn't take long to realize we had yet another problem. The eyelid spring didn't seem to work. When I lay down at night and blinked involuntarily in my sleep, the lid popped halfway open. That led to a few awkward moments when Nora thought I was staring at her in the middle of the night. But it also led to a dry and irritated eye that was red and swollen in the morning and didn't work very well. Through trial and error, we figured out that she needed to put Johnson & Johnson waterproof medical tape in the shape of an X over my eyelid at night, just to add to the horror-movie theme.

For the next six weeks, my days consisted of eating soup, then walking with a cane to an exercise bike, where I would work out off and on for several hours. Then I would watch a movie with closed captioning while my swelling went down.

I moderated the heat and ice treatments, even though "heat and ice, heat and ice," seemed to be the only advice the doctor in Beverly Hills would give.

A month and a half in, Nora and I realized that the eyelid spring had failed. My eye would open only halfway, where it would quiver as if I were about to wink at you or had just finished winking at you. Either way, I looked creepy. So we loaded back onto a plane for another five-hour flight to Los Angeles, took a cab to Beverly Hills, and got the same advice we'd been getting since the day we left. More heat and ice. I imagined Tom Hanks in a war movie leading his men against a much larger enemy. Between explosions, Hanks moves from one severely injured kid to another yelling, "Medic! I need a medic over here!" And our good doctor keeps showing up with a ziplock bag of ice and a warm washcloth. "Just alternate heat and ice," he tells each one.

Another six weeks passed. Now it was time to get back on the plane for another five-hour flight back to the House Institute to get my device turned on. Turns out my brainstem surgery had healed much faster and better than the silly eye spring, which we were beginning to think was a mistake. Nora scheduled yet another appointment with our Beverly Hills surgeon, fully expecting to get the same "heat and ice" we'd been hearing for three months. This time, he surprised us.

"I don't think it worked," he said.

There was a pause as Nora finished signing for me. Then I said, "You don't say."

We scheduled another surgery to adjust the spring. More blood, more thumbs-up through my paper peephole, more scalpels and sutures, which led to more swelling, which, of course, meant more heat and ice. The result of that one was that my creepy wink became a confused wink, with part of my eyelid at a forty-five-degree angle.

In total I had twelve eye surgeries, including two more to remove the torture device. There's probably a lesson here: when one of your three options in life is to go full pirate, give it some thought.

That third trip to California, though, had an incredible upside. I went to the audiologist at the House Institute for the final piece of the puzzle, the big reveal. Would Matt ever hear again? Had the brainstem implant hit on the right nerves, and would I pass the first, most basic test of auditory processing—the brain's ability to process the awareness of sound? In layman's terms, would I hear something? What I heard was irrelevant. Recognizing that sound existed was all that mattered.

This was years before the first-time hearing videos showed up on the internet, with all their heartwarming tears. Even if we had been sharp enough to film it, I'm not sure my experience would have gotten more than a few dozen hits. When I sat in the chair to have the device turned on, once again I did not know what to expect. I was anxious, of course, but I was also partially paralyzed, so I was limited in my ability to convey joy or disappointment. I watched as the audiologist put the device against the magnet inside my head. He then hit a couple of keys on his bulky laptop.

Just like that, I was immediately aware of sound.

"And we're back," he said. Those were the first words I ever heard electronically, and they terrified me.

Hearing had been a challenge for most of my life. Hearing something from the inside out is something few people have experienced and even fewer can explain. It's almost like one of those alien movies where the creatures communicate with humans telepathically. Their words just appear in the humans' brains. I could see the audiologist speaking. His lips were moving, and the movement corresponded to what I heard, but I didn't actually hear it in a normal way. It was as if the words came out of his mouth and were telepathically transposed into my brain.

Only the aliens got the software wrong. While I knew my audiologist had said, "And we're back," because I read his lips, what I heard sounded like a passing gravel truck.

That was okay. The surgeons had predicted that I might hear jackhammers or some electronic screeching. Dr. Brackmann had even used the words "gravel truck" to describe what the early sounds might be. The main thing was that I heard something. The electrodes were communicating with the auditory receptors in my brain. Sound was real again. Living with a rare and debilitating neurological disorder means, among other things, doing a lot of expectation management. Step one in this particular part of my journey was to live. I did that, and that was certainly a reason to celebrate. My ABI worked, in a gravel-truck sort of way.

That was step two, and another reason to celebrate. Managing expectations and celebrating wins where you can find them are the reason that even though moments along the way are hard, really hard, I'm able to move past the horror-film moments and enjoy the rom-com portions.

Nora was in the room with me and said, "Matt, can you hear me?" I immediately turned to her, my good eye wide and my winky eye still winky. Her voice, which I had come to recognize more than any other, sounded like a vacuum cleaner running over cat litter.

"Yeah, I can hear you," I said, and we both turned the stress of the last three months loose in a flood of emotions. My answer was also a bit of an educated guess. I mean, what else is she going to be asking me there? Her first words with my "new hearing" weren't going to be about tax law or thermodynamics.

"I love you," she said, signing and speaking the words together, as she had done for a while. The words came through like a distant shortwave radio signal clawing through reams of static. But it was still her voice. I could hear my wife again.

"I love you, too," I said. "It's not exactly crystal clear, but it's a start. There's a lot of work to do."

She smiled a bit, put both of her hands on my arm, and with a calm confidence said, "Matt, we've got this."

TWELVE

DON'T LET LIFE GET ME DOWN
GONNA TAKE IT THE WAY THAT I FOUND IT.
I'VE GOT THE MUSIC IN ME
I'VE GOT THE MUSIC IN ME.

—Kiki Dee

WATCHED A DOCUMENTARY ON THE EAGLES NOT LONG AGO.
Glenn Frey was talking about how he learned to be a songwriter, which I found fascinating. I had always assumed musicians and artists sat around quietly, maybe in yoga poses, until
inspiration struck. Then they hopped up and wrote down whatever brilliant epiphany popped into their minds. Some might
even yell "Eureka!" Frey dispelled that notion with an anecdote. He was a struggling musician playing rhythm guitar and

singing backup vocals for Linda Ronstadt at the time. He was also living in an attic loft apartment above Jackson Browne. Every morning while Frey was trying to sleep, he would hear Browne get up and put on a teakettle. Then Browne would head to the piano and work out a chord progression. The kettle would whistle, and the music would stop while Browne made his tea. Then the piano would start again, slowly, one note, one chord, and then a long pause before the next. Not long after that, the kettle would whistle again, and Frey knew that Browne was getting another cup of tea. This went on morning after morning, the same notes and chords and the same kettle whistling like a crowing rooster. The song Browne was writing was "Doctor My Eyes," which turned out to be his first hit and one of the most-played singles in his catalog.

"So that's how you do it," Frey said. No magic pixie dust, no lightning bolts of inspiration: just a hot cup of tea and hard work, grinding it out day after day until you had something you could polish and refine.

That story reminded me of something that happened after my first surgery left me in a wheelchair for months and then on a walker for months longer. Part of my early therapy had been riding an Airdyne bicycle, the kind with a big fan where the front wheel should be so the faster you pedal, the more air resistance you meet. It also had handlebars that moved back and forth with each pedal stroke so that your arms got a workout and synced up with your legs. This exercise was not designed to enhance my cardio, although it did that. The point was to retrain my brain and nervous system to connect the thought "pedal" with my legs and arms moving. It was also designed to get my body to remember a left-and-right gait again—right arm out, left foot down; left arm out, right foot down.

I had been frustrated with my therapy because it felt like the program was preset rather than adapting to my specific needs. For example, after that first surgery, as I rolled my chair into the room for day one of work at the rehab center, all I could think about was how this would be the path to get me up and walking again. I wore my Chicago Marathon finishers shirt and running shorts, and even traded slippers for Brooks running shoes, even though my feet would do nothing other than rest on those metal wheelchair footrests that day. Ready to get to work, I was pushed over to a table in the corner and handed a shoebox filled with rice and small buttons.

"Matt, you have about thirty minutes, try to find all the buttons without looking."

"Find buttons? With my hands? For thirty minutes?"

"Yes, but I understand if you need to take a break."

This was about to be the worst *Rocky* montage ever. What hype music do you play in your head for button-finding? "Itsy Bitsy Spider"? "The Wheels on the Bus"?

I sat there, discouraged. I don't want to be in the button-finding business, and I didn't see how this "rehab" was going to help me to do the things I wanted to do in life, like, say, walk again. When my button time had passed, the next station was placing and removing empty pans from a fake stove. Was this facility managed by Fisher-Price?

When Nora arrived for lunch with my Subway cold-cut trio, she was eager to hear how my first morning had gone. I explained my button finding and pan lifting. She shared my frustration and noted in an even but very determined tone, "Let me see if I can talk to someone about this." You do not want to be on the wrong end of Nora when she decides to "talk to someone about this." You've already lost, and the conversation hasn't begun. That afternoon, a different therapist showed up in my room. She was wearing her own marathon shirt and running shoes. Instead of pushing me into the rehab room, she walked ahead of me, bypassing the Uncle Ben's, and headed to the exercise bikes at the empty end of the gym. She and another therapist helped me onto a low Airdyne bike and told me to ride until I got tired. And I got tired fast, which she clearly knew would happen. The next morning we did the same thing, and each morning after that for a week.

At the end of the week, sensing my frustration that I wasn't seeing significant improvement, she said, "Matt, you are going to get through today." That was a very matter-of-fact statement, which was odd. It might have been the worst pep talk of all time. I thought that was the end of our conversation, but it turned out to be just the beginning. She then said, "But is that your goal? Is your goal to get through today? Or is your goal to get better today, tomorrow, and every day after?"

This was her way of saying, stop going through the motions. Either get better or go home, but don't waste everybody's time by doing this halfway.

I could get better by working harder, longer, and faster, or I could get through today. That talk ignited my competitive engine and changed my attitude about rehab. Like Jackson Browne at his piano with the teakettle on the stove, my work didn't have to look pretty. I didn't have to be inspired, or magical. I just had to do the work, day after day, inch by inch. Every goal in life that you turn into a reality comes through discipline, doing everything that is needed every day. That is true of songwriting, building a house, creating a business, or rehabbing from nerve damage after brain and spinal surgery.

You only progress by doing the work. I've come to avoid phrases like "shortcut" or "life hack," and even people who use them thinking it's a good thing. I have to earn it. I've learned I want to earn it. Otherwise, even if I end up with the thing I wanted, it doesn't mean what I hoped it would. When Steven Tyler sings *"Life's a journey, not a destination,"* I used to think it was a silly cliché. Now I understand that Steven had simply learned that lesson a lot sooner than I had.

In every one of those cases, work alone won't guarantee success. The songwriter you've never heard of who plays roadside nightclubs in Des Moines has probably worked just as hard as someone whose songs you know by heart, and the restaurant owner who fails in the first year might have put in a hundred hours a week. I had no assurances that the work I put in would bring feeling back to my legs. Nerve damage is far more fickle than Yelp reviewers. One thing is certain, though: if you don't have discipline and don't put in the work, you are guaranteed to fail. The only way to train yourself to be disciplined is to make the mundane work part of your daily routine.

I had to progress from that wheelchair to a walker. That required practicing my balance, by pushing myself into a standing position and holding on for dear life. There were falls, but that was part of the process. You have no idea how much your brain relies on feel until you can't feel a certain part of your body. I liken it to having your dominant hand in a cast. Have you ever shaved left-handed? How about brushing your teeth, or opening a doorknob, or putting a car in gear? Until you lose the ability to do those things the way you are trained, you have no idea how many motions are hardwired into your subconscious. The same is true for standing and walking. Millions of receptors in your legs and feet tell your brain, "Okay, my weight is centered, I have the proper amount of knee flex, my hips and spine are aligned, my quadriceps, glutes, and calves are all engaged, my toes are in the proper position, and I'm standing." This all happens by feel. When you can't feel anything below the waist, even though you can move, you don't know if your feet are in the correct spot, or if your knees are angled the right way. You get a sense of that when your legs fall asleep—I mean really asleep, as in beyond the tingle stage to the point where they are too numb to feel. Even though you still have nerves in your body sending signals to your brain, it's hard to know if your feet are making contact with the floor in the right way, and you stumble around like a toddler until the blood flow returns.

Multiply that feeling by ten and you are close to what my situation was like after that surgery. I couldn't feel my feet hit the floor or the legs that put them there. Too much weight on the outside of a foot and over I'd go. But each day, I would get on the Airdyne bike and push myself to go a little faster for a little longer. After that, I would hold myself upright for five minutes longer than I had the day before, even if it was mostly with my arms. Then I would slide the walker forward a foot and force myself to take a step to catch up. One step and then two, which eventually became a trip to the wall and back. Once I felt I had mastered the walker, I pitched it aside and went through the same process with a cane. I wished the rehab facility had one of those black lacquer ones with a diamond handle like Evel Knievel used to use, but I worked just as hard with a dull chrome one that had a rubber stopper on the foot and a hook for a handle. I set daily goals and then weekly ones, writing them down on the whiteboard or in a notebook I kept nearby. But the ultimate goal was 26.2 miles at a jogger's pace.

I had forgotten those lessons for a few weeks after my implant surgery. In my defense, my face was paralyzed, and I was running back and forth for eye surgeries on a more-than-regular basis. Plus, I had this new device in my brain that, when I turned it on, set off a grinding sound that did not travel from my ears to my brain, but seemed to come from the inside out.

My problem wasn't so much the paralysis, or the incredibly irritated and dry eye, or the fact that my balance was off again and, once more, I had trouble walking, or the new implant and the indecipherable racket it caused. The problem was managing all of those challenges at the same time while trying to be the husband Nora deserved.

As I've gotten older, I have come to the realization that multitasking is a myth. You can do more than one thing, sure. If you're a parent, you know that juggling multiple balls at once comes with the territory. But you can't master them all. In fact, it's almost impossible to master even one when a couple of others are barking for your attention.

Once we got home from California, my routine fell into a funk where I was "getting through today," and not even doing that well. For starters, I slept for twelve to fourteen hours. A big moment for me would be tying my shoes or maybe putting on pants with a belt. Some friends and coworkers likely wondered, "How can he lie around like that while Nora does everything?"

I get it. People's idea of brain implant surgery is like the old television police shows where a detective gets shot in one scene and shows up at the precinct in the next wearing a suit coat with his arm in a sling. Reality is quite different. If you've ever had surgery on a complicated joint—knee replacement or rotator cuff repair, for example—you know that recovery takes months. Now, think about the complexity of the human brain. Sleep was my body telling me to shut down while the mainframe rebooted. And since the body doesn't have an on/off switch, bringing all the systems back online takes more time than you think. I didn't want to sleep that long. I knew it seemed like I was being a slug. But in addition to a brain telling me to lie still, I missed the normal sounds of the day to wake me up. I couldn't hear the trucks on the road, or the dog walkers chatting as they meandered down the sidewalk, or Nora making breakfast. The auditory stimuli that tell you, "Hey, the world is up and moving, it's time for you to join," were not available to me. Thankfully, I had a wife who understood the biology of what was happening. There were times when Nora was frustrated, but she did a wonderful job hiding it. She let me sleep for as long as I needed to.

Once I woke up, I rolled out of bed and put on a pair of gray Champion sweatpants that I had cut off just above the knees. I also had a yellow T-shirt with two chocolate Easter bunnies on the front, one with a bite out of his tail and the other with a bite out of his ears. A bubble caption for the first one said, "My butt hurts," with the other rabbit responding, "What?" As deaf jokes go, that was a personal favorite. Then I would put the television on with closed captions and watch movies. One thing I discovered early is that if you put DirecTV on one-and-a-quarter speed, you turn a two-hour movie into just over an hour and a half, which was a neat trick when you considered that I watched four movies a day.

There were many days I would move from the couch to a chair early in the evening, just so Nora wouldn't think I had spent all day in the same spot, even though I had done just that. Every night she would come in from a long day of being the breadwinner and I would be sitting not far from where she had left me, watching *Anchorman: The Legend of Ron Burgundy* for the twentieth time.

The guilt I felt lying around while Nora played the part of caretaker and provider was enough to get me off the couch and onto an exercise bike for an hour every morning. It took some time and a lot of concentration to make sure I remained stable. But after finding my center, my legs and the pedals took on a life of their own. I drove myself to break that first sweat of the day, my legs driving like pistons and my breath and heart accelerating. As I got more comfortable with my balance, I pushed my speed and resistance until my thighs burned. It took a while before I felt good standing on the bike, but once I did, I imagined climbing Pikes Peak, racing against time and my desire to quit, pushing my lungs to process more oxygen and my legs to keep the blood flowing. I knew that oxygenated blood is good for your brain and that a solid workout would do wonders for some of the other problems I faced. But at that moment, I just wanted to get myself in motion again.

After the bike ride to nowhere, I would go to the kitchen and pick up a couple of cans of creamed corn. My surgeon had been very specific about how much weight I could lift. Two cans of Del Monte were right on the edge. Then I walked down two flights of stairs, turned around, and walked back up. I repeated that process until, one day, I realized that my balance was not back to normal, but to a point I would consider safe.

That was a win. And at that point, man, did I ever need a win. As gratifying as it was, I still felt a pang of annoyance. It was hard to celebrate a grown man doing things your friends' toddlers were pulling off every day. It was at that moment, in between steps while holding corn cans, that I began to formulate a new goal. It entered my brain to one day become the Midwest's slowest triathlete. After all, I had already run a 26.2-mile marathon, which was one of the legs in an Ironman race. The other two—swimming 2.4 miles and biking 112 miles—couldn't be that much harder, could they? Plus, most Ironman races allowed you up to sixteen hours to finish.

I wasn't sure when it would happen, but that day I decided I would do more than survive. I would thrive again. The world is blessed with great songs about running. Lyricists have run for the roses, have run with the devil, have run on empty, have run down dreams and taken money and run. But I wasn't running away from anything, so it was Bryan Adams's words that fit for me. *"When the feelin's right / I'm gonna run all night / I'm gonna run to you."*

The second goal was to restore some movement in my face. What I should have known at the time, and what thousands of years of human evolution has taught us, is that exercise to solve one problem often benefits other areas. That was the case with my new canned-corn training routine.

Friends who saw me during that time tried to be nice, saying things like, "Oh, you can't really tell you're paralyzed. It's not that bad," which wasn't even a plausible lie. If you get a bad haircut or chip a tooth, you might believe a buddy who says, "Don't worry, nobody will notice." But when half your face doesn't move, it's impossible to believe you don't stand out. The telltale sign was always how strangers reacted. An adult would see me and attempt to casually look away, as if there was something behind me that they were watching, maybe that unreadable sign fifty yards away, or that burgundy SUV stopped at a traffic light. If that didn't work, there was always the speck of dust on the shoes that must be examined and removed. I often felt like Roger Daltrey of the Who singing, *"Can you see the real me? Can ya? Can ya?"*

Kids certainly could. Just as I had experienced in the airport, my droopy lip, asymmetrical cheek, and eye that looked like melting wax sent shock waves through the minds of children. And they didn't mind staring. A few times when I ventured outside with Nora, a kid would walk up and say something, which I always assumed was "What happened to your face?" That was an innocent enough question, one that could have sparked a conversation about how, sometimes, people look different after something happens to their brain. The problem was, I couldn't answer because I couldn't hear, so the man with the strange face also ignored inquisitive children.

Then, one day after a solid workout, I felt something. From the day I had come out of surgery, I had rubbed my tongue on the roof of my mouth and along the gumline behind the teeth. This is what you do when you can't feel, as anyone who has had Novocain at a dentist's office knows. Only this time, I felt a slight tingle, almost like a new pimple was coming but hadn't quite formed. I knew there was something there, but the only way to describe it was "different."

Nora came home and we went to Panera Bread for dinner. With all the expenses associated with my recovery, and the fact that we were, at the moment, a one-income family, we no longer splurged on things like pasta primavera at Carrabba's Italian Grill. Panera was the sit-down dinner option of choice now. Plus, it had soups. Unless I got carried away, I wouldn't choke to death on soups, although given how my mouth operated, I might have chili chin for the rest of the night.

"I think I felt something," I said to Nora, slowly and quietly, continuing to work on modulating my voice so that I never sounded like I could not hear myself.

Then I proceeded to go through the facial exercises I had been working on since leaving the hospital—straining to raise a cheek or lift my mouth into something resembling a smile.

Every day I stood in front of the mirror in my living room or bath trying to will the muscles of my face to move. At the table at Panera that evening, I did the same. Only this time, Nora's eyes widened, and she said two simple words. "It moved."

Excited but not quite believing, I worked through the exercise progression again. This time, Nora leaned forward and said, "Matt. It moved."

No one has ever been as excited to rush into a public restroom in downtown Chicago just to look in a mirror. I leaned forward over the sink to get a good look in the mirror. Then I did my exercise again, pulling and tensing to get the facial muscles to respond. That's when I saw it. Just over the left corner of my mouth was the slightest movement, not a twitch or a tremble but an actual muscular response. I rubbed my tongue on the back of my lip, assuming, wrongly, that my earlier tongue movement had sparked this breakthrough. That didn't work, but it didn't matter. We had movement, measurable progress. We had another win.

Nora's anxious face met me the moment I walked out of the restroom. I nodded and the pools in her eyes spilled over and down her cheeks. Neither of us knew if this was the only motion I would ever regain in my face. But we had learned to relish small victories, and to celebrate every positive we could find.

My walking became running, and the stationary bike eventually gave way to the real thing. I even bought a Speedo and found a pool near our home. Through it all, I continued to work on my hearing. The more I worked with the ABI, the more

I could discriminate between sounds. I still couldn't understand much: the television, for example, would sound like a jackhammer on a metal floor while Nora's voice would sound like a four-cylinder engine about to throw a rod. It wasn't identification—I still couldn't tell you what either of them said—but I could tell the difference between the two.

Then, as I was running, I began playing the soundtrack in my head, over and over, as I had before. An hour into a jog and I could almost hear Bob Seger: *"Against the wind / I'm still runnin' against the wind / I'm older now but still runnin' against the wind."*

When I went home and, after several more months of recovery, eventually back to work, I was no longer able to manage my sales position in a way that was fulfilling for me or for the company. I wasn't on pace to hit my sales quota, a pretty big problem when that's essentially the only measure that mattered in that role. More than that, I wasn't able to be my best. I can handle losing business because a competitor offered a better solution but I was losing business because I couldn't follow phone calls or was too tired to catch a flight for an in-person meeting. I eventually assumed a new role in marketing that was more accommodating and less stressful—I listened for sounds that I could identify or recognize. Slowly, the discrimination got better.

With Nora, I began identifying the words I knew she was saying with the sounds my brain was emanating through the electrodes. Again, the sensation was weird. To call it hearing was almost wrong, because hearing implies sound coming in and being funneled through a channel to the brain. This process was sound being interpreted by an electrode and coming from the brain back out. Still, when I knew Nora was saying, "Matt, I need you," or "I love you, good night," or "Pass the salt and pepper, please," I could identify those words and phrases with the new impulses I was getting. I was relearning language and communicating through sound. At the time I had no idea that I was developing a skill an audiologist would one day compliment me on, calling it "superior predictive analysis." It was like one of those brain teasers where letters or words are missing, and you have to fill them in—*Wheel of Fortune* without Vanna or the ability to buy a vowel. I was an Olympian in that sport because my life revolved around filling in the blanks.

On one of my long, quiet, and ultimately selfish training runs in the fall, when the weather was cool enough that my mind could shift to topics other than "Why am I running again? I'm so bad at this." I began to reflect on the things I would miss the most if my hearing never improved past this stage, like my family saying, "I love you."

Sure, I had some wonderful songs in my head, classics that are staples in a lot of people's memory banks. But I had been told that I would never hear a new song. Music was relegated to what I remembered from before and what my ABI could restimulate in my brain. That meant I had lost one rite of passage. Every aging generation deserves to be able to turn to the kids and say, "Turn off that racket. You call that music?"

Why couldn't I have those moments? Why couldn't I have

some of the bonds that new music brings between family and friends?

On that slow fall run I decided it was time to get off the mat and fight back. I went home and I put in that slightly scratched CD from the center console of my old Honda Pilot, the one I'd listened to for years before my hearing loss. I peeled a Werther's Original off the label side, breathed hard on the playing side, and wiped the breath off onto my sweatpants. The gold CD made by Maxell had letters printed in my hand with a black Sharpie: "songs we like." I put the CD in the car stereo and turned up the volume. There, through the miracle of ABI, I listened to my Honda belt out the sound of gravel trucks for twenty minutes. This, I decided, would also become a part of my training.

What I couldn't have known was that it would make triathlon training seem like kindergarten recess.

At the time I wasn't sure that getting your hearing "back in shape" was even a thing. But I couldn't come up with a good reason not to try. Rocky Balboa punched sides of beef to get in shape. All I had to do was move my index finger eighteen inches and press play. "Eye of the Tiger," baby.

I listened to those same twelve songs, songs that I knew and could hear in my head. The 2006 Honda had an advanced feature that showed onscreen what song was playing. That was my cheat sheet, my hint as to what I was hearing.

Day after day, I let myself be serenaded by the soothing sounds of those dark gravel trucks. But on a day no different from hundreds of others, I got into the passenger's seat of Nora's Jeep Liberty, and she backed out into the alleyway from our apartment in downtown Chicago. Typically in a car, the sound of tires on the street, the air-conditioning on low, and the mix of big-city sounds means everything is just noise to me. As I looked out the window that morning, the background cacophony of sound was unexpectedly interrupted. The words, *"Johnny, what you doin' tonight?"* came from the door speaker.

They were far from clear, but I definitely heard those words. Nora was about to turn the music down so we could talk like we normally do. But I grabbed her wrist and asked nervously, because I didn't know what to do next, if I was right. "Is this 'Crazy Game of Poker' by O.A.R.?" I asked.

That was a band we liked and had seen at the House of Blues several years earlier and was part of Nora's collection of CDs stored over the passenger side sun visor.

"Yes, it is," Nora said. Then the weight of her answer registered on both of us.

She pulled the car over and we hugged as best we could while still wearing seat belts.

I heard music. This wasn't memory. This was hearing. This was something experts had told me I would likely never do again. People who knew more about ABI than anyone else in the world had said this was nearly impossible. And yet . . .

I heard music. Not a song in my head; this was music playing at the moment in real life.

The magic of that moment was the feelings I felt I had regained. When you think about the music you love or the special times associated with a particular song, the memory probably includes the people with you at the time, where you were and how you felt about them. Some songs trigger memories so vivid you can see smell the air from the past and see a friend or loved one from long ago.

I had accepted that music was something that was only going to be replayed in my head. I would be the sole listener, alone with my memories and the feelings they brought along. I never imagined a scenario where music would become a social interaction again.

We listened to the rest of the song and I didn't catch even one other word. Then we listened to the rest of the album, and I didn't hear another song. But it didn't matter. Because I heard music. And that's a really big carrot on a really short stick for a deaf guy. It was the motivation I needed to keep practicing, to keep working, to keep listening.

A year later, I could catch a refrain from two or three different songs on my "songs we like" album.

"Ohhh, we're halfway there, oh-oh livin on a prayer . . ."

"Don't cry, don't raise your eye, it's only teenage wasteland . . ."

"Feelin' good was good enough for me, good enough for me and my Bobby McGee . . ."

It was worth the hard work every time. I was starting to see the very small measurable progress in my hearing that I had remembered seeing with my walking.

There might be science to back this up now. At that time, it wasn't available. But music became hearing therapy for me. For years sound came to my ABI in a way that the human brain had not evolved to process. I was asking my brain to bypass the entire natural hearing mechanism and just figure it out on its own. There was no road map; at best, it was a *Goonies*-style map left in an attic, dusty, stained with a very unlikely promise of treasure.

The doctor had told me that the goal with the ABI was to hear oven timers. For real, oven timers was the example I was given. With that in mind, after a few years of work, my brain heard oven timers. But after that, my brain and I said, "Why can't we do more?"

There were times when my brain said, "Nope, it's oven timers and gravel trucks from now on, pal." Even the professionals, the smartest people in the field of ABI technology, said, "Wow, you're hearing oven timers and gravel trucks. That's amazing." But I continued listening to the same songs over and over again.

I updated my ABI program annually, but the changes I perceived were minimal. I continued to process out-of-focus sounds in the same way. But on that one run, that one day, my brain casually mentioned to my ABI, "Hey, pal, I've been meaning to bring this up for a while, but there's never the right time. I appreciate all that you do for me, and the oven-timer thing really was pretty cool. For a few years now, you've been telling me that other things like voices and songs sound one way, but I have this sweet mix tape I've been listening to here and it's telling me something different.

"I remember what some of these songs are supposed to sound like. And that is not what you're telling me here."

From there, through practice and repetition and confidence, my brain started making this case to my ABI more often. And each time, the case grew stronger.

My ABI pushed back, saying, "Look, pal, I've got twelve electrodes and gave you a sense back. I'm doing the best I can do here. You're asking me to paint a Monet with three generic crayons. I can't do it."

I listened to more music and my brain prepared more arguments. "I'm telling you, Paul McCartney is saying 'Mother Mary' right there, and you're trying to tell me he is saying 'Mhhhmmmmhhr.'"

Over time, my ABI begin to relent. The implant started allowing me to process sound the way my brain remembered. "Mhhhmmmmhhr" became "MthrMry." "MthrMry" eventually became "MotherMary." "MotherMary" eventually became "Mother Mary comforts me."

Slowly, methodically, and sometimes painfully, "Mother Mary comforts me" eventually became "Mother Mary comes to me."

And one day, after all that work, I was listening to the Beatles instead of recalling the memory of listening to the Beatles.

Instead of catching two or three words from two or three songs, I started missing two or three words from every two or three songs. Music became my Rosetta Stone, translating the language my ABI was hearing into the language my brain knew how to speak.

When I first started to hear music, there was a sense of accomplishment. I had worked hard to get here. But there was also disappointment, because the words and tunes didn't sound the same as they had in my head. I wrestled with those feelings, because I knew how lucky I was to hear anything at all. But it's difficult to relive the emotion from a song or a lyric when you hear it in a different way. After trying for so long to hear, when I finally could again, I almost felt like I was faking it.

Then something dawned on me. Even those who hear perfectly don't feel the same way today when hearing a song as they did twenty years ago. The memories are there, but the feelings change. It's called maturing.

We hear with our brains, not our ears. But we feel with our hearts and souls. Those parts of us grow wiser, more understanding, and more caring as we age. Whether you hear music with ears or through mechanical means, your feelings will evolve over time. That is how it should be.

I have a playlist on Spotify now. Once I feel I can really hear a song again, it gets a permanent spot. The list is now sixty-six songs long, and they are some good ones.

When I say permanent spot, I mean it. I lost something I love and never thought I'd get back. We're probably all living each day with a hole in our hearts created by losing someone we love. They're gone, and our only real option is to move forward and adapt to a life without them, hoping the hole will get a little smaller. But it rarely goes away completely. As months and years pass, you might struggle to remember what a person's voice sounded like, the way they laughed, or the way they made you feel. Those losses hurt in a whole new way.

Now imagine a decade later, you walk into a doctor's office

and see that person standing there, smiling, arms out, waiting for you. Sure, you'd freak out, but you'd also hug that person as long and as tight as anyone ever has. You'd never let them go again. You wouldn't want to let them out of your sight. You'd probably repeat over and over, "I can't believe you're really back in my life."

Well, I can't believe music is back in my life. Now that it's here again, once a song is added to my soundtrack, I'm never letting it go. So while my playlist will continue to grow as I continue to refill that hole in my heart, songs will never get deleted.

I'm never letting them go.

The soundtrack I had memorized became my starting point, the key to taking me out of rattling gravel trucks and back into the world of the hearing. Don't get the wrong idea. This wasn't a miracle. I didn't walk outside our place and hear birds chirping clear as day. That might never happen again. Most of the sounds I experienced after that still suggested metal scraping on metal. But music became my linchpin, the program to translate the language of digital impulses into sounds a human brain could understand.

I pulled up the songs on my playlist, the ones I had kept close for the history they had played in my life. At the time I'd committed them to memory, I had no idea that they might be the boards on the bridge that brought me back: *"Like a bridge over troubled water / I will ease your mind."*

Some were easier to pick out than others. My AM radio dial

would move back and forth around a familiar but distant sound. I picked up Tom Petty's voice for some reason, not because of its distinctive timbre but because the of the unmistakable beat at the beginning of "Runnin' Down a Dream"—"*Workin' on a mystery / goin' wherever it leads.*" Wailing guitars and a strong backbeat made it easier to segregate sound through the static. Simple, repeating lyrics came quicker—"*Tuesday's gone with the wind*"—and songs that I had memorized in childhood seemed to be clearer—"*Your love is like bad medicine / Bad medicine is what I need*"—although I'm sure that was just a trick of the brain.

My motivation for embedding those songs into my memory bank was never to forget the emotions they triggered. Now, they were helping me to take the next step in my journey, discrimination and identification: not just hearing, but hearing something that I recognized from before.

Listening to these songs with Nora, the music that had been a part of our journey, felt like a miracle. Not only could the deaf be made to hear again, but through the trials and hardships, the love of my life was still by my side.

THIRTEEN

AND NOW MY LIFE HAS CHANGED IN OH, SO MANY WAYS
MY INDEPENDENCE SEEMS TO VANISH IN THE HAZE.
—The Beatles

DON'T GET THE IMPRESSION THAT EVERYTHING WENT BACK TO NORMAL ONCE I HEARD MY FIRST ABI-ENHANCED SONG. Retraining the brain isn't that quick or easy. No one who has experienced nerve damage after having tumors removed bounces back by the end of the week. To this day, I still struggle with partial facial paralysis, and I still hear things in fits and starts. AM radio static defines much of my hearing experience, even with the latest technological advancements. I have adapted in many ways, including practicing my facial movements so that my paralysis is harder for people to notice.

In the early days that was not the case. Even after our breakthrough moment in Panera Bread, when I could feel my gums against my teeth and Nora noticed a little movement where there once had been none, I worked for months just to move my mouth into something close to a normal position. Having it work the way it should was a yearslong exercise.

Those days strained every part of our lives. We were never broke, but when you go from being a two-income household with a mortgage and a twice-a-week restaurant budget to being a one-income family with eye-popping medical bills, stress becomes real. Plus, we both were, by nature, social people. Despite having hearing loss for most of my life, I had never had trouble engaging with old friends and making new ones. Complete deafness coupled with facial paralysis complicated every aspect of our lives. Not only did I feel cut off, but I had spent almost a decade preparing for my eventual deafness with the idea that I could still communicate through lipreading and facial expressions. But expressiveness is a two-way street. I'd never planned for one lane of that road to be blocked.

During that time, Nora and I did our best to remain social. As is the case with most couples, we went through a period when it seemed like we were invited to a wedding a week. We attended as many as we could. They were wonderful ways to keep up with old friends and meet their new spouses and extended families, plus we got to dress up and eat well, but maybe now we'd have to sit out the chicken dance (which is great, because all I ever want to do at a wedding is sit out that stupid dance). Every time we put on our best party clothes for a wedding, I always had the same thought: My wife is incredibly hot. Yes, she was kind, intelligent, empathetic, giving, loving, wholesome, and talented, but she was also one of the most attractive people I'd ever seen. Seeing her put on the dresses she set aside for wedding season affirmed it. I had outdone myself on the marriage front.

When we would attend weddings, the age-old social scenario would begin to unfold where the men and women split into two groups, the men hanging out by the bar and the wives and girlfriends congregating somewhere near the cake without it looking like they know they're by the cake. Once segregated, the guys would catch up on work or reminisce about adventures of the past. Invariably, someone would say to me: "Matt, is that Nora over there?"

Hearing some noise that sounded like "ora" and "ere," coupled with lipreading, and knowing the context of the question, having heard it more than a few times, I would say, "Yeah, that's her in the blue dress."

To which someone else would say, "Wow, dude, she's hot."

I often imagined a similar conversation going on between the women at the cake table. "Hi, Nora, where's Matt? I've been dying to meet him."

"Oh, he's there at the bar, navy suit," Nora would say.

To which the woman might respond, "Oh, is he . . . drunk?"

"Oh, no, that's just how he walks because of his balance."

Another woman, perhaps not a friend and jealous of how Nora looked in that blue dress, might then say, "Is he a pimp?"

"No," Nora would say with the patience of a saint. "He carries a cane because he tends to fall."

Another friend, who might be genuinely concerned, would follow with, "Is he okay? He looks sad."

Nora would no doubt say, "Yeah, he's fine, he just can't move that half of his face very well because of nerve damage. It's tough for him to smile or show a lot of emotion."

They would go back to talk of the gifts and the venue and how it couldn't have been a prettier day for a wedding. Then another woman might say, "Is Matt listening to a ball game or something?"

Nora would then say, "Oh, no, that's his new surgically implanted hearing device. It makes it possible for him to hear sounds. He can't understand much yet, but he can at least hear something."

Then the jealous woman, maybe an appletini or two into the afternoon, might say, "Wow, he seems so great."

I'm sure that sort of thing didn't actually happen, but the thought that it could, or at least the certainty that similar thoughts ran through the minds of many of our friends, is what drove me to take the extra step each day to work on my balance, go through the painstaking facial exercises, and continue to work on my speech so that my voice never jarred anyone. There is certainly nothing wrong with deaf people speaking in whatever way they wish—it is laudable that many people who cannot hear themselves communicate well through the spoken word—but I added speech drills to my daily routine. It would be some time before I added swimming and, eventually, running.

No matter what they are, health issues make you focus on yourself. You become insular. It's nature's way of keeping you alive. In olden days, if you caught a cold and continued to go out to gather food, it might become pneumonia and kill you. Becoming self-absorbed during times of illness has made sense throughout all of human history. But when you have a long-term problem, one that will be with you for the rest of your life, you figure out a way to make yourself better while making life good for those around you.

I had more than myself to consider. I devoted myself to personal improvement and worked to get better every day for my wife, for her future, and for the family that we hoped to build. I didn't sing it out loud to her—in part because I was deaf, but also because I was never a great singer—but I often hummed and often thought about Kenny Loggins's classic "Danny's Song."

"And in the morning when I rise / You bring a tear of joy to my eyes / And tell me everything is gonna be alright."

We both wanted children. That was not unusual for a couple our age—it might have been the most clichéd feeling in the world—but when the feeling hits you for the first time, it's easy to think you are the first human to have an urgent yearning to perpetuate the species. It hit me perhaps a little harder than most because of how I had faced my own mortality. I didn't want to have kids in the "I can't wait to chase the little rascals around in the park" kind of way. I wanted them in the "I might not live until the end of the Cubs' season" kind of way. I wanted my family name and my connection to Nora to live on for generations, and that created a sense of urgency in building a family. Years from now, whether I'm there to see it or not,

I want people to look at my children and say, "You have your mother's eyes," or "Your father had the same bad golf swing." Whether or not I lived to see another birthday, I wanted to fill our home with little people. That way, if, God forbid, I passed in my sleep, Nora would have the pitter-patter of feet to remind her of our time together. My friends and family wouldn't have to rely on low-res images from a Motorola Razr phone when they thought of me. Instead, they could call the kids into the room and put them on their laps.

The first question we both had to answer was "Can I even do this?" That's a question a lot of prospective parents ask themselves as they go through the family-planning process, but for us, there was a little more to it. This wasn't run-of-the-mill self-doubt. I didn't realize it at the time, but I'd already fallen short of a vow I'd made to Nora just a year prior (no, not the fidelity one: it turns out lack of facial movement keeps one's eye from wandering both literally and figuratively). I'd promised to be there for her in sickness and in health. To me, this meant a commitment to being there for her if she got sick in the same way she was there for me. But where I failed her was that I wasn't there for her during my sickness. The rest of her life didn't just stop because I was unhealthy. She was dealing with the loss of my hearing, the unexpected loss of a close friend, and the painful loss of a loved one. I was so wrapped up in trying to get through each day that I couldn't give her the support or space she needed to deal with other darts life threw at her. If I couldn't be there to support the most independent person I know, how would I ever do that for a baby who was completely dependent all day, every day?

This NF2 journey was far from over, given that my tumors would likely return and I would require more surgeries, with additional risks. Was it fair to bring children into the world when their father might die too soon? Then there was the question of what I could and could not do as a father. When these discussions first began, I had just had my hearing restored through a magnetic disc attached to my head, and even with that modern marvel of science and technology, most things still sounded like an old dial-up modem. I had also just recently learned to walk again, but most of my balance was still visually based. The idea of carrying a child in my arms, given my risk of taking a spill, did not give either of us good feelings. Nora had just spent a year dressing me, and I wasn't too far removed from a diet of soup, much of which ran down my chin every time I ate. My dear bride had cleaned up after me, translated for me, and driven me everywhere I needed to go. Children are a full-time commitment with two able-bodied adults. Was it fair to anyone for us to even be considering parenthood?

Throw in the fact that we were just reigniting the honeymoon stage of our marriage—a time that had been delayed because of brain surgeries and those family tragedies—and it was easy to talk ourselves out of the whole idea of building a family. We were in our late twenties, relatively new owners of a Chicago apartment with a view of the Hancock Center; I had just gone back to work, so we had reliable income from two relatively stable paychecks; my hearing was bad but getting better; and our social lives were picking up at a healthy clip. As young homeowners with some doctors' bills to pay, we went out carefully. There were a couple of places where we could get half-price wine and a tavern nearby that offered free wings and salad after 8:00 P.M. on Wednesdays. It might not sound classically romantic, but in our minds we were living the life a Bon Jovi cassette tape sold us in the fourth grade: "*We've got to hold on to what we've got, it doesn't make a difference if we make it or not. We've got each other and that's a lot for love.*"

We were on the cusp of being able to afford a trip to a Michelin-starred restaurant every so often. It would be nice not to need to arrive early and sit at the bar to take advantage of the happy hour menu. We could take vacations and actually fly places like Vail to ski, or Italy to see some of the most beautiful historical sites in the world. I thought about all of these trivialities and more. When I could drive again, I might want a cool car, not a minivan. We might want a vacation home in the mountains instead of pouring money into a college fund for the kids.

The pull to spend time with each other was strong, but so was biology. The more we discussed our future, the more we realized that we wanted a family more than we wanted stuff. Tater tots and tacos made a fine dinner, and we could drive five hours to ski the hills of Michigan if we wanted.

Finances and my ability to change diapers at night were not all that concerned us, though. NF2 is genetic, which meant I had up to a 50 percent chance of passing the disease on to any biological heirs I might bring into the world. NF2 can happen spontaneously, as it did with me; neither of my parents had NF2, but this is incredibly rare. However, if either parent has the faulty gene that causes the disorder, there is a one in two chance, a coin flip, that the child will be born with NF2. Bringing a baby into the world when you know that you could be transferring a life-threatening disease presents you with moral and ethical questions that most couples in their twenties would struggle to answer. My parents had never heard of neurofibromatosis type 2, or merlin, the tumor-suppressing protein my faulty gene failed to produce, so the questions we were asking had never occurred to them. How selfish is it to want a child so much that you risk giving him or her the disease that has caused so much turmoil in your own life? When I looked at myself in the mirror and saw my partially paralyzed face, knowing full well that the outcome could have been worse, how could I take a heads-or-tails chance of passing that on to my children?

Nora, being the medical expert and most logical thinker in the family, summed up our options. "The choices are no kids, adoption, a surrogate, in vitro fertilization with genetic testing, or we cross our fingers and hope for the best," she said.

I didn't put much faith in the fingers-crossed method. I was someone who had a 1 percent chance of facial paralysis when the anesthesiologist said, "Have a good sleep," but who was rolled into recovery facing a year's worth of follow-up surgeries, dietary restrictions, and exercises to regain some facial movement. Taking a fifty-fifty chance with my child's life was not a risk I wanted to consider.

That's when I realized what an awful hypocrite I had been. Without realizing it, I had often questioned the choices people in my life had made concerning family planning. Gee, why did they choose to adopt? Or why would that person consider a surrogate? What is the deal with in vitro anyway? At the same time that I thought those things of others, I shook my head at people who said, "Well, it's God's will," when it came to family planning. We are people of faith, but I have always believed that God did not give His children large brains and the ability to reason by accident. In my mind, making rational, moral decisions is God's plan. And when things get fuzzy and the right answers aren't obvious, you do the best you can with the information you have. Now, embarrassment and shame filled me like a tanker at the fact that I could hold both those judgments at the same time. Who was I to judge the choices of others when it came to their families? Those who trusted the Lord to make their family plans might end up with a small tribe of children on a budget I could not comprehend, but so what? That was none of my business. Just as I had no cause to offer an opinion on families who chose IVF or surrogates, or those who chose to become foster parents or adopt children, either domestically or from faraway lands. Nor did I have the right to pass any judgment on those who chose not to become parents at all. Now that I stood on the same path as those whose lives I had inadvertently judged while speeding by, I felt a hot tingle rise in my ears. That was a mistake I would not make again.

In the meantime, Nora, as she had with every other aspect of our health and well-being, began researching genetic testing and in vitro fertilization. To be fair, she did go to med school with an eye on working in genetics, so she understood way more than I did before we ever logged on to the internet through our ancient browser. Our first search for "Neurofi-bromatosis Type 2 baby" yielded exactly one hit, an old pdf from a London medical journal. The summary jarred us. Very little clinical data existed on babies born with NF2 because the life expectancy for those diagnosed with the disease at birth was thirty-two years. If I fit into that life-expectancy category, I might be dead before our child attended kinder-garten, which brought us back to the first round of questions. Was this the right thing to do?

Our searches for IVF stalled at that point. We shut down the computer having learned that a little bit of medical infor-mation is a dangerous thing.

After a couple of nights of sleep and more chats through our familiar combination of ABI sounds, lipreading, sign language, and charades, we began the search anew. Nora went back to the internet, hoping to find something in a peer-reviewed medical journal, while I reached out via email to my contacts at the House Institute. I couldn't have been the first NF2 patient who had questions about parenthood. That as-sumption was correct. My friends in California fielded ques-tions about family planning all the time, and in most cases, they laid out the statistics that we already knew—the coin-flip analogy of passing along NF2, and that babies born with NF2, on average, didn't make it to forty. However, those conversa-tions led Nora to finding an article about a researcher at Mass General Hospital in Boston whose focus was on NF genetics.

Nora reached out by phone, explained our situation, and after a lot of voicemails, explanations, and re-explanations, she got the answer we wanted. The researcher, a woman who was sympathetic to our plight and anxious to help, would study the genetic makeup of my tumors and see if there was a way to minimize our risks through IVF. This sounded like a dream scenario, but it was also tinged with another stab of pain. None of this research was cheap. We had health insurance, but genetic testing for family planning purposes isn't covered by most policies. Thankfully, we had just enough savings to cover the gap, although it hurt my heart to know where we'd gotten it. Tom had owned enough life insurance to keep Sarah comfortable and to give Nora a nice boost. A year after his passing, Tom continued to help his family, present and possibly future. A grandparent's gift to the grandkids he'd help make possible but never get to meet.

Once we filled out a flurry of insurance forms and signed a stack of agreements, the House Institute boxed up a slice of the tumor they had taken from my brain and shipped it to a basement office on the other side of the country. From there, the researchers went to work. Nora would call on a weekly basis to check in, and I could see some of the notes she was taking. They included phrases like "ezrin-radixin-moesin" and "cortical actin filament C-terminal," along with words like "mosaic," which was the only one I recognized, even though I had a feeling that in this context, it didn't mean what I thought it meant. At this stage, I let the adults do the talking. Nora would fill me in when I was needed. The process was called preimplantation genetic diagnosis, or PGD. After reading my genetic map, the doctors could fertilize one of Nora's eggs in a dish and watch it "grow up" until it was five cells old (so few "five cells old" card options at Hallmark). The clinician would then remove a single cell and compare its genetic map with my own to confirm whether NF2 was present.

Once the researcher finished with the complexities of her study, isolating this protein and segregating that filament, Nora and I were recommended to one of the leading reproductive health facilities in the world, one of fewer than a handful with a track record of success working with NF2 patients on in vitro fertilization. It was called the Reproductive Genetics Institute, a name that hit all the right buttons for us. I especially liked the fact that the name was English, meaning it was located in a country where I spoke and understood the language. Catching every third or fourth utterance with an ABI and then piecing the puzzle together with context doesn't work when the words are French. But after beating a trail back and forth to Los Angeles for my implant and eye surgeries, we were prepared to go to Tasmania if that's what it took.

To our shock and pleasant surprise, we finally caught a break. Not only was the Reproductive Genetics Institute not in some far-distant land; it was just a few blocks from our home, on Halsted Street in Chicago. We rode past it a couple of times, because it was tucked between a Walgreens and a KFC, not exactly the address you expect for a cutting-edge genetic research facility, but it took only one meeting for us to understand the process. As the sperm donor, my "contribution" was easy. As had been the case in our relationship from the beginning, Nora did all the heavy lifting, including injections, more injections,

larger injections, setting timers, being sedated for egg retriev-
als and again for egg transfers.

After again reviewing the genetic hoops they'd be helping
us jump through, the doctors noted that we had a reasonably good shot at a viable pregnancy. The original terminol-
ogy for IVF was "test tube baby," although the fertilized eggs
were never in traditional test tubes. Regardless of the verbiage,
Nora and I, through the miracle of science, did create two embryos that were confirmed with a high degree of certainty to
be negative for NF2 and on hold at the Reproductive Genetic
Institute. The news of two embryos was of course wonderful,
but there were still a lot of steps before we could allow ourselves to think about a future with "the twins."

Many times in that process, I played one of the Elton John
songs on my soundtrack, ostensibly to work on my hearing,
but mostly for how it made me feel as we worked through the
weighty questions before us. *"Oh, Daniel, my brother, you are
older than me / Do you still feel the pain of the scars that won't
heal?"*

D octors put our chances of a successful pregnancy at above
average, because, with that one rather noteworthy exception, we didn't have any other health issues that might impede
fertilization. Still, the odds were 40 percent, give or take a small
margin of error. With that in mind, we implanted both embryos and waited on a bed of nails to see if they took. Once the
children were growing, at our final meeting with the reproductive geneticist before being transferred to traditional OB/

GYN care, the doctor gave Nora what remains the most back-handed compliment I have ever heard. "Your wife has a very accommodating uterus," he said without cracking a smile.

Unsure how to take that, I simply said, "Thanks?"

The next eight months were like waiting to be hit by a train. You are on the tracks. You can see it coming. It keeps getting bigger in your field of vision, but it seems to take forever to arrive. Johnny Cash was right. I could *"hear that train a comin' / It's rolling round the bend,"* but when or if it would hit was anybody's guess.

Nora carried the twins almost to full term. We welcomed Luke and Maddie with all the joy of all first-time parents. Luke arrived weighing just over seven pounds, and as he let out his first scream from a head of blond hair, I told Nora, "We have a son." She looked back at me and made it clear with one simple statement that the celebration would need to wait a beat, as her mind and body still had an immediate focus. "I have to do that again." Luke's sister took her first breath a few minutes later and just a few ounces lighter. But as with many things in our life, every celebration was tinged with a hint of dread, not exactly of impending doom, but a back-of-the-mind fear that the next shoe was about to drop. The first twenty-four hours of the twins' lives, as we waited for the results of the blood drawn from their tiny feet to confirm or rule out the presence of NF2, were the longest I had ever spent.

For the first time, I knew what my parents had gone through on the multiple occasions they had waited with me: the anguished hours they had spent in hospital waiting rooms, the dread they felt when the doctor came out with news. Worrying for your children is an order of magnitude worse than going through procedures yourself. My appreciation for everyone in my life grew in that long day. They had gone through more than I knew.

Doctors came in carrying paperwork. Nora held the children, one in each arm. He looked at the papers and I wanted to scream, "Tell us!" The expectation was that the tests would be negative, but I wasn't supposed to have been in a wheelchair for months after my surgery, either. It couldn't have been more than a couple of seconds before he spoke, but it seemed like an hour. "I have good news," he said, and I felt my knees buckle. The results were negative. The science had worked. We had two healthy children, with no signs of NF2.

That afternoon we celebrated with Dairy Queen Blizzards and a healthy cry, as you do.

I quickly latched on to the joy of sharing a birth story that ended with "IVF with PGD at RGI by KFC so no NF2."

FOURTEEN

WHEN A MAN LOVES A WOMAN
CAN'T KEEP HIS MIND ON NOTHING ELSE
HE'D TRADE THE WORLD FOR THE GOOD THING HE'S
FOUND

—Percy Sledge

WORRIED EVERY DAY FOR NINE MONTHS, FIRST OUT OF FEAR THAT DESPITE ALL OUR EFFORTS, THE KIDS WOULD BE BORN WITH NF2, BUT ALSO BECAUSE THE LIST OF MY LIMITATIONS WAS ABOUT TO GROW EXPONENTIALLY. That is why I implore everyone I speak to, whether at a conference or in a one-on-one setting, that when you see a couple with one partner who is deaf, or blind, or has some balance troubles, perhaps multiple sclerosis or a neurological issue like cerebral palsy or even Parkinson's disease, please understand that this is not a minor inconvenience for the un-challenged spouse. It is their life. Driving, cooking, working, changing lightbulbs, taking out the trash, lifting laundry baskets: each seems minor in a vacuum. Compounded, day after day, these tasks are like a slow drip on the forehead.

Nora had taken care of me during all my NF2 surgeries and setbacks, but she had known about my condition from the day we met. I had been transparent about my limitations and what might lie ahead, so as a couple we had entered our marriage knowing what could come. That all changed with the birth of the twins, and when it did, the "Can I do this?" question was answered, "Yes, I can," but only because of Nora. The guilt overwhelmed me.

One child is a handful. Two are organized chaos. Twins can plunge you into perpetual exhaustion. Early on, Nora decided to breastfeed for as long as possible. Two days in, I thought "as long as possible" would be forty-eight hours. Every new parent knows that babies get hungry every three hours, which means the parents never get enough REM sleep. What few people tell you is that twins don't always wake up to eat on the same schedule, and they don't start eating the second they awaken. Nor do they fall back to sleep the moment they stop eating. Without a good burp, you might get no sleep. Add poop into the mix and you have a full night. That process repeats on a loop, seven days a week, twenty-four hours a day. It takes about four days for parents to understand why the CIA uses sleep deprivation as an enhanced interrogation technique.

Every mother of a newborn looks frazzled. Mothers of

twins have a special room in heaven. Our evening routine once I got home from work was like a well-choreographed play. Sometime around 6:00 P.M., Nora would feed Luke while I got Maddie warmed up in the on-deck circle. Fifteen minutes later, we swapped. Nora fed Maddie while I changed Luke and got him all swaddled up in his crib. At six thirty, Nora would hand Maddie to me and I would put her in bed next to Luke, who had been crying for a solid fifteen minutes by that point. Another fifteen minutes of stereophonic crying and they were usually both ready for yet another diaper change, after which they fell asleep around seven thirty, and we had peace and quiet for an hour or so.

At 9:00 P.M. the process began anew. This ninety-minute dance repeated eight times every twenty-four hours. During daylight hours, I could help. I could burp them, swaddle them, swap them, get them to bed, and get them up. The night was different. I can't sleep with my implant receiver on, and once it's disconnected, I wouldn't hear a grizzly bear in the room with us. So Nora set an alarm to punch me, so that I could get up and pass her little people. But before I could get up, I had to put the receiver back on behind my ear, which takes about thirty seconds to find and make comfortable, assuming the batteries are charged, a minute or so if they're dead. That doesn't seem like a long time until two infants are wailing like sirens at 3:00 A.M. Then it seems like a year.

The other serious problem was that I still needed to see to control my balance. Vestibular nerve damage never fully heals. I rely on visual cues to keep from falling. That's fine in the daylight hours or when the lights are on. But in the dark, it was dangerous for me, and potentially catastrophic if I was carrying one or more babies.

The third problem was that, for all its technological wizardry, the ABI has limits. It can process sound, but discrimination is up to me. Background noise is unfiltered and overwhelming, so when I had two crying children in a dark room, it was like being in a gunfight in a dungeon. My limited ability to help, coupled with the short fuses that always come from lack of sleep, led to some resentment and blame, which was completely understandable. More often than not, Nora would get up and do it all herself, which underlined my fears that I couldn't be the father and husband they deserved. Despite my best effort to carry some of the load, an exasperated "I'll just do it" became her mantra.

If I couldn't provide the basics to the kids at night, what could I provide, really? Throw in the fact that I couldn't be left alone with them at night—if something happened to them or we had an emergency, I would sleep right through it—and I began to question my value as a man. It sounds macho, but protecting the family is the minimum every man expects of himself. Without that, I really did think *"my independence seems to vanish in the haze."*

The wonderful and heartbreaking thing about kids is that they grow. Once they sleep through the night, you miss those tiny infant days. Then they roll over, crawl, and before you know it, you're locking the cabinets and putting bubble wrap on every sharp corner in your house. Then you look back on pictures of the chubby cheeks when they could only sit up, and you wish those days hadn't flown by so fast.

Even though my hearing improved as I continued to adjust to the ABI—from the ol' gravel trucks to fax machines to radio static, with a song or two thrown in to keep me on my toes—the toddler phase brought a new set of challenges. A typical night might include a 3:00 A.M. wake-up with Nora's elbow landing in my ribs. With that as the typical middle-of-the-night method of jolting me awake, I had to hop up and be ready for everything from a fire to masked intruders to me hogging the covers. Once semi-awake, I would say something: "What's up?"

Nora would answer with something like: "Maddie has been crying for hours because she dropped her pacifier, and I've been in there six times, crawling under the crib to get it, but now she thinks it's a game and is throwing it on the floor to get me to come back in. She's also trying to wake up Luke to play the pacifier game. I can't go back in there."

I might then say, "Sorry, my batteries were dead. What'd you say?"

Nora never complained about carrying an outsized load in our family, but the words "never mind" cut like a blade, no matter the context. While the speaker might mean, "Oh, never mind, I was just babbling about nothing," I would hear, "I have been trying to engage you and I'm simply exhausted now, so never mind."

As the kids grew, and we taught them sign language, life became a touch easier for everyone. The twins mastered it quickly, in part because young people absorb new languages as easily as they change clothes, but it helped that we taught them at a time when American Sign Language was trendy among suburban moms, so books and tips on learning it were easy to find.

Our life was not like others, but it became comfortable for us, so much so that two years after the twins, we did it again. We revisited the same IVF clinic, this time knowing what to expect. While we love being the parents of twins, it wasn't something we necessarily needed to experience a second time. So we gambled on that accommodating uterus of Nora's and implanted a single egg, with the same 40 percent chance of success. Nine months later, Kate arrived and wrapped up our family of five. The phrase "bundle of joy" might be a cliché to some, but it's an accurate description of Kate since the moment she came into the world. I remember the "oh, poor me" attitude I had about the additional challenges we'd have to face to have a family. Now, with the clarity hindsight often brings, I realize that we tried to get pregnant exactly twice ever and have three healthy kiddos. I try to remember this anytime NF2-related issues weigh on me.

Two years later, driving and working and still struggling with the seemingly never-ending eye thing, I reached one more goal. At that point I had a few of the small life wins under my belt, but they still felt like wins in the context of "for someone with a physical disability." I needed a win that didn't require context.

With three young kids and a wife who should have been nominated for sainthood, in the prime of my life except for the fact that I can't hear without an implant, can't see without glasses, and still need a cane for balance, why not finish that final goal of competing in a triathlon?

A quick Google search should have taken me to a page that just said, "Dude, no." Instead, it took me to a page that offered a thirty-six-week comprehensive run/bike/swim training program that required twelve to eighteen hours a week of aerobic activity. That should have been the first flashing red light. For starters, when I began the process, I needed help getting onto a bike because of my equilibrium, not to mention the partial facial paralysis and, oh, yeah, being deaf. But there was also the fact that I was working again, at a real job that required a lot of my time and attention. And when I wasn't working, I had young twins and a baby at home. A thinking man would have said, "Yeah, this is a great idea, but maybe another time." Instead, I did some math. I figured I would need about ten weeks of training to be able to start at week one of that thirty-six-week program. That put me at forty-six weeks, not quite a full year. Other than all of that, this was going to be great.

I felt sure Nora would agree, after changing the baby and getting the twins fed. If I had asked her opinion on this life-altering decision, she most certainly would have patted me on the back and said, "Go for it, big guy" But I didn't ask. Instead, I figured I would train, get it all over with, and sit down with her in eleven months to say, "Surprise, I'm in an Ironman."

In all seriousness, what I did not realize at the time, and would not accept until much later, was the fact that I was not training for a triathlon to satisfy some lifelong dream. As a kid, I had never seen myself as an endurance enthusiast. My athletic accomplishments, modest as they were, had become a replacement for the things I had lost. Many men instinctively compensate for a loss through replacement. A man loses his hair and takes up tennis, or he gets arthritis in his knees and suddenly shows an interest in automotive repair. It's a story as old as history, from a man losing his wife and taking his nation to war to a guy in Chicago losing his hearing and competing in a 140.6 mile Ironman triathlon.

Not having a long conversation with Nora about this was an awful decision, one of the most selfish I have ever made. She was supportive, at least in the beginning, although there were times when I would leave for a run and see a wistful glimmer in her eye. She worked, too. We had small children. I'm not sure if she saw me doing something for me instead of doing something for our family, or if she sensed the quiet desperation in my new obsession that I somehow missed. Either way, she continued to run with me on occasion, although she had no interest in expanding into triathlons.

What I didn't contemplate at the time, because, again, I was compensating for a loss, was the fact that a forty-eight-week training program for a triathlon put a heavy strain on our family. At the time I thought, This is great. I'm not just recovering from all the awful stuff that's happened, I'm thriving, and raising money for NF2 in the process. What could be more noble?

The answer was: staying home and paying attention to your family, doing the small things like rolling around on the floor with the kids, or feeding everyone, or simply being there. It was a hard lesson, and one a lot of people miss. I have to admit, Nora shut me out and became distant during that time. Why wouldn't she? When she needed help, when we wanted to communicate, I was on another seventy-five-mile bike ride or heading out for a swim. At the time I thought she was wrong to feel the way she did. In hindsight, I'm embarrassed by that. Competing in a triathlon was my attempt to regain something I felt had been robbed from me. Not my hearing, or my facial movement, or my equilibrium, but my manhood. What I didn't know then and do know now is that you can never get back what you've lost. Not totally. The time, the tears, the opportunities: they are gone forever. What you can take is the lessons and the love that came from out of your loss. That, in the end, is how you move forward.

Nonetheless, the forty-six weeks of training came and went, and race day finally arrived. I confess that I was really worried about race day. With Grandma Lasbury watching the kiddos at home, Team Hay arrived in Sandusky, Ohio, on Saturday evening for the usual waiting in lines to get a race number and to weigh in. It's the first sign that you are in for a long day that you are required to get on a scale ahead of time and have your weight monitored throughout the race.

I also had to drop off my thirty-five-pound recumbent trike at the staging area, a spot where bikes that cost more than our last two cars combined were lined up like Ferraris at the starting line in Le Mans.

The next morning, I hopped up at three thirty for breakfast, which is a lie. No one hops up at three thirty, ever. It's the middle of the night, the hour when sane people are in their deepest REM sleep. But that is the time triathletes eat, because to push breakfast back any further would mean eating too close to the swim start, a guarantee that one's breakfast will be seen again at some point.

After a good meal and a short break for some stretching, we headed to the beach behind the hotel at six thirty for a seven o'clock start. Nora, my crew chief, came to see me off and offer some great advice, like "Stop talking, they're having a moment of silence." What would I do without her?

Then we hit the water, the first and often the most difficult leg of an Ironman, and certainly the part that keeps a lot of people from even attempting a triathlon. I felt solid on the 2.4-mile swim. It was probably my strongest long swim ever, with each of my splits being exactly where I wanted, allowing me to finish right at my one-hour-thirty-minute goal.

When my bike ride started off well, I began to replace my worry about not finishing with thoughts of "I'm really doing this." Knowing I still had a lot of pavement ahead, I pushed myself at a steady 75 percent of my capacity. That plan worked fine for the first half of the ride, a distance I had ridden dozens of times in training before coming home to make pancakes or go watch a T-ball game. But around mile 60, a long hill was topped with what is called a "false flat," meaning it looks flat, but it's still a hill. The false flat is just level enough to make you question why you can no longer break the 15 mph mark despite your best efforts. If you've seen the movie *Ghost*, you may recall the "bad spirits" being represented by nasty shadows that creep up on the bad guy. That is exactly how I felt. I could feel the shadows of passing mailboxes and "Sweet Corn" signs creeping up on me. Those shadows carried with them thoughts like "You still have fifty miles of biking and a marathon to run" or "Now you see why Lance Armstrong didn't ride a recumbent trike in the Tour all those years." These are Did Not Finish thoughts.

The last bit of advice I got before race day, other than "Stop talking, they're having a moment of silence" was to stay in the moment. Up until mile 63, I thought this was a "Stop and smell the roses" thing that people just say, sort of like "It is what it is" or "Just do it." Shame on me. Staying in the moment got me to mile 64. Thoughts of all the folks with NF2 who had reached out to me got me to mile 65. Recalling all the support from friends and family got me to mile 66. And the most wonderful downhill coast got me to 67.

The 112-mile bike leg wrapped up as I pulled back into the corral seven hours and twenty minutes later. My crew chief was standing there to greet me with smiles after having spent the day braving the roller coasters of Cedar Point as a single rider. I knew I wasn't feeling well when I stood up off the trike, but I don't think I realized how bad I was until I saw the way Nora was looking back at me and heard the way she spoke. Because of our time together, even though hearing her was still a challenge, I understood the subtle difference between "Doing okay?" and "Matt, are you okay?" The latter is especially important to note when you have a rare, debilitating neurological disorder.

So I did what any responsible person would do nine hours into an Ironman. I lied. I told Nora that I was fine.

As I changed shoes for the 26.2-mile run, I let myself forget the live-in-the-moment rule and take a second to think "I'm totally going to be an Ironman today."

It was a strange thing to be working out as the sun rose and still be working out as the sun set, knowing I had ten more miles to run before the event was over. My biggest worry about the sun was that I still tended to fall in the dark, not like a standard stumble that could happen to anybody, but a fall where I didn't realize I was falling until I hit the ground. Fortunately, the run was in downtown Sandusky, and there was quite a bit of street lighting.

Throughout the run, I ate nothing but GU gels. I had cut out caffeine in the weeks leading up to the race, so in addition to the thirteen hundred calories I got from the gels (taken every other mile with water, with Gatorade in between), I felt like I had bonged a pot of coffee.

At mile 22 my trusty crew chief was there to meet me. In some ways this felt like my finish line, because now I knew there was no way I wasn't completing this thing, which is exactly what you tell yourself right before you fall and break an ankle. By the time I had only four miles to go, I had gone a full fourteen hours without my implant on, so as Nora and I spoke, I'm pretty sure every aid station volunteer was thinking, "Why is he yelling at that nice girl?" I'm not sure how much sense I made at the time, but I remember her suggesting that I start running instead of walking (now that's a crew chief), and I remember her calling my dad for me. I'm not sure that I have ever worked harder at anything than I did training for this race, and I wanted to let the guy that taught me about hard work know that I was about to finish.

Nora told me that "Eye of the Tiger" was blasting as we approached the finish line. I'm glad it wasn't a song written in the last decade, because I could at least sing this one in my head. *"It's the thrill of the fight / Rising up to the challenge of our rival."* After a six-hour-and-twenty-minute marathon, we were able to cross the finish together at the 15:42 mark. I had my finish-line picture.

I don't know what I expected to feel when I crossed the finish line, but it was a rare mix of emotions. I was too tired to feel pride and too proud to feel tired. The days of being mistaken for a pimp were behind me, at least for now.

When the twins were young, we went to a lake in Kentucky, one my parents had taken us to when we were young. It was a relaxing weekend, a time when all of us could stretch out and unwind. One of the first things I did when we got there was put a life vest on Maddie and plunk her off the boat dock and into the lake. I jumped in right behind her. But there was a problem. My legs weren't working well enough at the time for me to tread water. It wasn't that I couldn't tread water well, I couldn't do it at all. Within seconds I sank like a cow. The only thing that saved me was the strap on Maddie's life vest. Right before plunging below the surface and almost certainly drowning, I used my daughter's life preserver to save my own.

I thought about that moment after my triathlon. I had grown up spending my summers on the water. I water-skied, wakeboarded, tubed, swam, and anything else you could imagine on a lake. The fact that I almost drowned just a few feet from a dock drove home an old saying I read somewhere: A healthy man wants a hundred things. A sick man only wants one.

I would never hear the way I once did, and never move my face in the way I did before. More surgeries are likely to yield different results, some good and some surprising. But, for now, I have the one thing that I want, the one thing that matters: I have the love of a family and the ability to love them back.

Sure, I miss some things. Poor hearing means there are a lot of unknowns. Maddie and I now tell the same joke minutes apart, with me thinking it's original and wondering why nobody laughs. As a curious toddler, Luke would ask wonderful questions that should be asked more often, like whether cats enjoy climbing stairs. I miss these in real time and have to rely on Nora to provide me with the greatest hits from the day.

The time I miss hearing most is when I'm running the carpool to gymnastics, dance, or baseball. When kids pile into the back of an SUV, they tend to forget that an adult is behind the wheel, and they share all kinds of things with each other. It's like a Jane Goodall moment, except instead of studying gorillas in their native habitat, you have a load of boys in the back of a Subaru. If I could hear them, I would learn who is kind, who is empathetic, who is the bully, who is the alpha, and how my own son fits into the mix. Instead, I hear static and the occasional lyric from a song on the radio—"*The cat's in the cradle and the silver spoon . . .*"

I also missed a lot of opportunities at work, in part because of the long absences when I was hospitalized or recovering from surgeries, but also because hearing loss made it difficult to move up the corporate ladder in marketing when I often had to wait on transcriptions or rely on lipreading during presentations. I saw a lot of colleagues whom I had surpassed before I lost my natural hearing who were now several positions above me. For the longest while, I had trouble identifying how I felt about that. I wasn't jealous of what my work friends had accomplished. They were professionals who had done a good job and deserved everything they'd earned. But I felt left out, and isolated.

Once again, music helped me clarify that feeling. As I was listening to music on the television with closed captioning, an Elton John song came on and I read the lyrics and I sang along. That was one of the keys to training my brain to sync with the ABI. If I repeated words that I heard as they were being said, the brain recognized whatever sound the ABI was making as that word. So if I had the text of a speech that was about to be delivered and could recite the speech along with the person giving it, my brain would hear those words from both me and the speaker while the part of my brain that reads would associate the sound with the word.

In this case, the lyrics were familiar, and the tune was fantastic. *"I'm growing tired, and time stands still before me / Frozen here on the ladder of my life."*

I stopped when I read and sang those words. That was it. Those were the words to describe my work life. Time stood still before me while it moved on for everyone else. There I remained, tired, and frozen on the ladder of my life.

That realization might have thrown some men into depression, and it certainly did not make me happy. But I had my priorities in order. Nora grew more beautiful by the day, and I was thrilled to hear the kids say, "Eww," when I told their mother that she was hot. And the kids knew that even if I missed hearing some things, at least I was there. Like a lot of things with hearing loss, I focused on what I could hear and not what was missing. There will always be gaps, blanks, lonely moments of absolute silence. Then, out of nowhere, I'll hear two syllables that shine a bright light into the world—"Hey, Dad."

Sometimes those two words are the prelude to a question. Other times they are a greeting, and sometimes a singsong conveyance of annoyance. No matter what, I hear them, and they bring me back to the most important things in life. My kids know that hearing requires my undivided attention and total concentration. They understand that I am not listening in on their conversations, so if they need to make sure I'm hearing something, they preface it with "Hey, Dad," and I'm all in. What follows is not always important, but what happened to get us there is always magical. "Hey, Dad" is an invitation into their world, a place where I don't often listen in, but one where I join every time I'm invited.

Both my girls wanted me to sing them to sleep at night when they were young. Because of my limited repertoire, I had to pick wisely. "Blackbird" was always a good one. "The Ballad of Curtis Loew" was hard to beat. After a while I settled on the Eagles. I had all ten songs from their first greatest-hits album memorized in a way that I would never forget a single word, but I also had to do a little age-appropriate editing at times.

When Maddie was old enough to change the car radio on her own, she stopped scrolling on "Peaceful Easy Feeling" and her eyes got wide. That's when I realized she had never heard the song sung by anyone but me. She even kept the edits in place without realizing it. *"I like the way your sparkling earrings lay / Against your skin so brown / And I want to sleep by you / in the desert tonight / with a billion stars all around."*

Years later, when our youngest, Kate, also wanted to hear my singing, she would say, "Daddy, sing the U2 song." That was "All I Want Is You," and I would tune up. *"But all the promises we make / From the cradle to the grave / When all I want is you."*

Fast-forward to the first grade, when I was carting Kate to another bouncy house birthday party. Lo and behold, "With or Without You" came on the radio and Kate said, "Dad, are those the same people who sing the U2 song?"

That was about the same time that Kate said, "Hey, Dad, I think I want to learn to play guitar, can we . . .". Before she finished the question, I was already searching for the best guitars for kids. From the day they were born and pronounced healthy, I had an irrational fear that lack of musicality was an inherited trait, like eye color and the length of your toes. Even when I could hear, I couldn't play anything, and my singing would earn me more than a few side-eye glances. Still, I grew up believing that nothing was cooler than a campfire and somebody grabbing an acoustic guitar and strumming a simple A, D, D, A, E chord progression before launching into some Tom Petty: *"She's a good girl, loves her mama / Loves Jesus and America too."*

By the time I'd finished shopping, I had found compelling reviews for the Taylor GS Mini. We ran out to our local guitar store, where I pulled the mahogany Mini off the stand and was about to convince my six-year-old that we needed to over-spend. When I looked up, she had picked up the store brand and said, "Hey, Dad, can we get this one? It's yellow."

"Well, the mahogany Taylor GS is a much better guitar," I said.

"Is mahogany yellow?"

I heard all of that, and it will stick with me for the rest of my life, long after I have forgotten that a first grader saved me three hundred dollars and I was sort of disappointed.

Not long after that, Kate took her series of guitar lessons that ended with a recital at a Lutheran church, where Nora and I sat in the front row. Of course, I thought Kate won the thing until Nora told me that it wasn't a competition. After-ward, as we were leaving, I said to Kate, "You were so cool up there. I wish I were able to hear the music a little better."

She shrugged and said, "That's okay. I just like that you're here."

Just like that, I had a lesson in the things that truly matter.

In case I needed reinforcements, at Luke's first Little League practice, I showed up to be an assistant coach, which I thought would be perfect. I didn't have to make schedules, do lineup cards, worry about uniforms, or meet with parents. I would teach kids how to catch and throw a baseball. What could be better? Unfortunately, I was running late from work, so I showed up to the first day in a suit and loafers. "Hey, I'm Matt, Luke's dad. How can I help?" I asked.

The head coached looked me up and down and said, "Are you the GM?"

I was after that, at least in nickname.

"Head out behind second base and shag any balls that get through," he said.

A lot of balls got through. The head coach hit them way too hard for nine-year-old kids to field, so I found myself chasing baseballs through the grass. Then the coach yelled at me, "Hey, GM,————, right?"

"What's that?" I asked, turning and leaning in, hoping to catch it.

"Just————, thanks."

That left me in a pickle. Should I guess? Should I ask him to yell again? Just as I was about to run in and explain to the coach that I don't hear very well, Luke looked over his shoulder and said, "Hey, Dad, the coach said take those balls in the field and hit some pop flies to the outfielders."

It was a minor moment, something most people would have forgotten before dinner, but for me it meant everything. From the moment we had first discussed becoming parents, I worried that my hearing loss would be an embarrassment to my kids or make me less of a father, and as such, less of a man. "Hey, Dad," vanquished those fears forever.

I've also learned that worry hampers advancement. My dad would add some Indiana wisdom about worrying and say, "That and fifty cents will get you a Coke." There's no value in worrying about the things I can't control. When I memorized my soundtrack, one of my motivations was a fear of losing the songs that connected me to people and memories in my life, but I was also afraid that I would never be able to hear any other music again. Even with artificial hearing, experts say that the music you hear is the music you remember. New stuff sounds like noise.

I am living proof that this isn't wholly accurate. Most of the music my kids listen to sounds like chain saws to me, which makes me sound like every parent who ever wandered into their child's room when the stereo was too loud. In my case, that isn't an exaggeration. Some of the stuff Nora tells me is quite good sounds like a bottle cap in the garbage disposal. But not all of it.

One day Nora and I were taking a spring walk through a park near our home. As usual, I hummed a tune as we walked. A few steps in, Nora grabbed my arm and said, "What are you doing?"

"I'm humming," I said.

She nodded and smiled. "You're humming 'It's Hard Out Here for a Pimp' by Three 6 Mafia."

"Yeah," I said, not getting it yet.

"Matt, well, first, odd choice, but second, that song wasn't written when you lost your hearing. You aren't remembering it from before. You're remembering it from now."

Once more, we cried together at just how far we had come.

FIFTEEN

EVERY MARRIAGE HITS ROUGH SPOTS. How our marriage went as long as it did without them is a question for the ages. But just before we turned forty, we realized that we were living our lives in parallel universes, like business partners who had two corner offices at opposite ends of the floor. We could see each other. We were operating in the same sphere, but we were always just an arm's length away, close enough to appear great from the outside, but never close enough to be right with each other. We were two adults sharing the same house, but we were on autopilot. It was difficult to process. I didn't know how we'd gotten there. We didn't just wake up one day with a different relationship, but it sure felt that way.

When your car runs off the road, you don't abandon it. You pull it out and fix it. Relationships with the people you love are far more important than an automobile, even an expensive one. I knew that Nora and I needed to do something to turn us back from an unhealthy time, but I wasn't sure what that entailed. Even though we both admitted our marriage needed work, we weren't committed on a regular basis to fixing it. Without that commitment, an external catastrophe could send things off the rails, and no one wanted that, especially with three young children.

It turns out that an external force helped instead of hurting, and it came out of the blue. Both of us were given work opportunities that allowed us to move to Indianapolis. My job went virtual, with occasional travel, and Nora was able to work and travel out of the center of Indiana, our roots. Chicago is a wonderful town, and we built the best of our lives there, but we were Hoosiers, descendants of sturdy corn-fed stock who felt at home the moment we moved back.

A few years earlier, we made the cliché young parent migration from the city to the Chicago suburbs for better schools and a yard. That move meant more square footage and an attached garage (with a second refrigerator . . . Chicago burbs love the second fridge), but it also added a ridiculously long commute, which sometimes had me gone from 7:00 A.M. until 7:00 P.M. The opportunity in Indiana brought with it the luxury of my being home to help get the kids off to school and be home when they arrived back in the afternoon. Once the kids hit the school bus, Nora and I had an hour together in the morning. Because we were new to the neighborhood, we didn't know anyone, and the neighborhood had some wonderful walking paths. We also had a small dog named Ollie who was borderline incontinent. To keep him from soiling the carpets in the new house, Nora and I spent our morning hour together walking the dog a mile and a half.

We realized that it was the first time in years that Nora and I had more than a few minutes without each other either running in or going out. We realized again that we had things in common, that we thought the same way about a lot of things, and that we could chat and enjoy being around each other. That led us to rekindle a friendship in addition to our marriage. There was never a time when I thought we might go our separate ways—we are both too stubborn to let something that important fail on our watch—but we also recognized that with the kids pulling us in every direction and our careers demanding more of our time, finding moments with each other could not be accidental. So we scheduled time together, most of the time to walk the dog, but occasionally to go out for lunch while the kids were away.

Those dates led to deep conversations where we voiced concerns that had been building and festering between us. Once they were out in the open, we realized that the effort needed to fix them wasn't that monumental. A silent problem always creates more problems than one aired for all to hear. Within a couple of months, we realized that the two of us were friends again, which was the start to bringing the entire family closer. We had been like the Pink Floyd song, *"Two lost souls swimming in a fishbowl, year after year."* Now we were high-fiving in the kitchen again, which we needed because our lives were about to take yet another unexpected turn.

When you've worked for the same company for nineteen years, a portion of your identity is wrapped up in the culture of the place, but also your goals change. There is a reason you don't find many people who work in the same place from age twenty-one to forty. What I realized, though, was that by year nineteen, I was staying for the money and insurance, which, despite what you hear in marketing seminars, is not a terrible reason for taking and keeping a job, especially when you have a wife, three kids, and a serious health condition that requires frequent trips to specialists. People take jobs they don't love all the time, because loving the job isn't as important as loving work and the value it gives you. The money and opportunity my longtime employer gave me allowed me to do a lot of volunteer work for NF2 research and other hearing-loss organizations. My job filled my wallet while my volunteer work filled my heart. I likely would have stayed right there if that option had been available.

During a video call in 2019, a manager in New York whom I had never met let me know that I had been "downsized" and no longer had a job. It was about as awkward as possible, because I used a closed-caption service to transcribe calls in real time, but no matter how good they are, there is a slight delay between the person on the other end saying something and me reading it. So, right after the New York guy said that I had been laid off, I said, "Hey, I know we've never met, but the transcription service has a little bit of a delay, and . . ." At just that point in the sentence, the words "you've been downsized effective immediately" flashed across the screen.

I said, "Well, this call took an awkward turn, didn't it?"

I looked for work for the better part of a year, every day and in aggressive ways, meeting people in coffee shops and bakeries and in offices, wherever I could find them. For the first time in my adult life, I was out of work. And, unfortunately, there wasn't a huge demand for deaf forty-year-old marketing and sales managers in Indianapolis who had one company on their résumé.

With the search continuing, Nora and I took the kids on a planned ski trip to northern Michigan. We went to a family-friendly resort where all the lifts arrived in one area, making it convenient to find the kids when needed. I wasn't panicked on the job front just yet, although concern was setting in.

Then divine providence reached out again, this time in the form of a fall.

I'm not a good skier. If walking was a problem for a long time for a person with no functioning vestibular nerve, finding the edge of a ski while zipping downhill at extraordinary speeds was silly. But I gave it the old college try despite falling a lot. So, while trying to follow my eleven-year-old down one of these Michigan slopes, I fell, having just removed my hat to soak up a little sun. When I hit the snow, my implant receiver fell from behind my ear. I lay in the snow with one ski dug into the hill, took off my glove, and plowed through the snow with my hand searching for the thing. It took about twenty minutes for me to find it, panic growing deeper with each passing second.

Once I found it, it was saturated from having been submerged in snow. And it did not work. I got nothing—no beeps or long tones, just silence. I found Nora and told her what had happened. Then I went back to the hotel and tried the oldest and worst trick in the book: I stuck it in a bowl of rice. Of course, that didn't help. Then I tried the bathroom hair dryer, and I tried changing the batteries. Nothing worked.

After four days of silence on the slopes, we returned home, and Nora made an emergency appointment with my audiologist. In the meantime, we went back out to walk the dog and ran into a neighbor. Nora explained that I couldn't hear at the moment because my implant receiver had gotten wet—thankfully, she didn't describe my wipeout on the slopes or my frantic digging like a groundhog looking for it.

Our neighbor's eyes got big, and she said, "You know I'm part of a cell phone retail company, right? Well, we just bought a company that dries cell phones when they get wet. Many of them can be saved. The guy who invented this tech wants to take it to the hearing aid industry and dry those. Matt should go see him."

It was only a fifteen-minute drive, so I went to see what this was about. Normally, when my implant had gotten really wet in the past, it was at least a one-week process to send it back and get a new one. A nice man named Reuben at this company called Redux looked at my implant and said, "Oh, yeah, we can dry this out really quick."

He put the device in a machine for twelve minutes. When

Reuben took it out, he seemed thrilled, and I felt sorry for him because I was sure it wouldn't work.

I put the implant behind my year expecting to hear nothing. Instead, I heard crisper, clearer sounds than I had heard in a year. Reuben saw the look in my eye, smiled, and nodded. "Twelve minutes, total moisture removal," he said. "We do it every day."

And just like that, an untapped service to provide care for the hearing impaired became my mission. I mustered up the courage to ask if they were hiring and gave my best pitch on why my personal and professional background might be a great fit for launching their technology in hearing care. I left their office with a handshake for a position as director of audiology sales. I'd spend the next three years working for Redux, touring the country to bring their innovative solution to hearing-care professionals while speaking out on behalf of the hearing impaired.

In the meantime, I heard another song that wasn't on my list. It was Lady Gaga and Bradley Cooper singing "Shallow," which was written well after I lost my hearing. Once again, the fact that it was in a movie, so I could see the words while hearing the music and watching the performance, must have helped. After that, I added the song to my list, one of two "newbies" that I have in my library.

Losing a job and some divine intervention led me to a career that aligns with things I care about and understand on a personal level. I found a place where the things I learned throughout my NF2 journey could make a positive difference.

Advocating for better hearing care with the Redux team helped me to find my voice and gain confidence in using that voice to improve the patient experience.

My crayon box hasn't gotten any bigger. I still have the same three colors. I've just learned to craft works of art with them, to use all available information to train my brain to do things my doctors did not know I was capable of doing. Because of the love of my wife and my beautiful children, I am still fighting for all those who feel trapped in the silence. I hope to be their soundtrack and do for them what so many people have done for me.

While I was writing this book, my dad, Ken (Kenny to those who knew him best, and Mr. Hay to the two generations of students who made apple-shaped cutting boards in his shop class during his thirty-year teaching career), passed away. He was not a complicated man. He wanted green beans and mashed potatoes and to sit in the same row at the eleven o'clock church service every Sunday. He used to say, "You might outluck a Hay; you might outthink a Hay; but I'll be damned if you're ever going to outwork a Hay."

Dad was tough but fair, and devoted to my mother, my brother, and me. We got sideways a few times. I thought that the lessons he hoped to teach and points he tried to make could have been done with a few less cords of firewood split, or one or two fewer lawns mowed, and maybe not so many driveways shoveled when the snow fell in Indiana. Fortunately for me, Dad was right.

He taught us how to safely unhook a fish; he taught us how to track a deer; he taught us how to change the oil in the car and change the tire on the side of the road at night. Those lessons and so many others helped prepare us for the rain life can sometimes bring to your picnic. He didn't take a single weekend trip without inviting us.

His five grandkids grew up knowing a man who was easy to laugh with and even easier to love. And he taught until the end, lessons fewer kids are given today—when all else fails, use a worm and a bobber; never touch a trigger until you're ready to shoot; and always lift with your legs, not your back.

His passing is worth sharing here, because of the fight I put up throughout the years of surgeries, nerve damage, and rounds of recovery. Matt Hay did not learn on his own how to come back from partial paralysis and vestibular nerve damage to compete in an Ironman. Those were things he learned as Ken Hay's son, who was irrationally persistent and who nobody was ever going to outwork.

My long and winding road has come full circle. When I first got my ABI, I heard again, but the racket was indescribable. The more I've learned and the longer I've been at this, the more I know that humans can retrain their brains to do amazing things. When we first hear as children, a certain section of the brain says, "Okay, I'll take the hearing part," and nine steps are devoted to converting waves into an identifiable sound. By implanting an ABI, we have short-circuited that process, adding a tenth step and bypassing a few on the front end. The brain is not ready for that when it happens. But it can be made to change. Just as we can grow, and develop, and change in everything that we attempt to do.

Dad used to always say, "Never be afraid to ask questions. Too many people are because they don't want to look dumb. But asking questions is how you learn about anything and everything." He didn't say this at a seminar or onstage at an event. This was a Tuesday in our town. He dispensed that sort of advice all the time, and on most fronts, he was dead right, especially about being curious and quizzical. If you don't ask, you'll never learn. That's true of everything from your medical care and the care of those you love to the price of a yellow guitar in the storefront window.

My time at Redux was valuable in ways well beyond a paycheck. After years of feeling limited by my hearing loss and doing all I could to work around it, that role showed me there was real, even if accidental, value in what the previous twenty-five years had taught me. Rather than hide that education, I now had the confidence to leverage it. So when the FDA approved the first drug ever to treat certain types of NF tumors, something we'd been fundraising for going back to Nora's first marathon the year we met, the pharmaceutical company that developed the drug began recruiting a team.

This large company specializes in rare diseases, but since there weren't any other pharma treatments available, they were searching for someone who knew NF, knew the NF community, and knew the patient advocacy groups that support them. After several conversations that were increasingly exciting, I agreed to serve as their U.S. director of advocacy for NF. My job is to represent the voice of the NF community.

It took me over two decades to find my own voice. Now I have the opportunity to help others do the same. In the nearly quarter century since I got my diagnosis and my ABI, the technology has advanced so far that it is conceivable that NF2 patients will one day live and hear as well as they did in their younger days. I get to work toward that goal every day.

In the meantime, I will also coach baseball and take the family on vacations every chance we have to get away. My beautiful wife, Nora, remains the backbone of our home, a fiercely independent woman who continues to do more for her family than anyone I know.

The songs still play. I hear them and sing to them—not well, but that was never the point. I was able to embed the music of my early life into my brain as a time capsule. Now that I have opened it, my hearing and appreciation of music are better than any of my audiologists could have imagined. But then, when I turn off the implant, sound evaporates like a vacuum in space.

Every day I give myself a pep talk about how my hearing loss doesn't have to limit what I'm capable of doing. Those conversations used to take hours, then minutes, and now, just seconds. But they still happen. Every day. They're shorter because I no longer feel *"frozen here on the ladder of my life."* I have no interest in trading *"all my tomorrows for a single yesterday."*

I do think about the life I've lived so far compared to the lofty vision a younger, healthier me had of how things would go. I believe that kid would be surprised and pleased that it's been the obstacles we have overcome and the joyful, albeit slightly crooked, smile on our face that has defined us.

Paul Simon, the closest thing I have to a favorite poet, perfectly described the current state of my soundtrack. *"The vision that was planted in my brain still remains / within the sound of silence."*

ACKNOWLEDGMENTS

I love movie soundtracks. *Stand by Me*, *When Harry Met Sally*, *Dazed and Confused*—there are a hundred more great records of songs directors selected to help them tell a story. The music referenced in this book, however, wasn't chosen after the fact to help. These weren't jingles to help move a story along. The songs referenced in these pages—and, believe me, I know there are a lot of them—were all part of my story, my life, as it happened.

It would be hard to separate my memory of an event from the music that played behind it. That was the premise of this book from the beginning. Music meant more to me than it might have to others because of the long path I took to losing it, and the miraculous journey I traveled to find it again.

I don't know how to properly or sufficiently express my gratitude to the songwriters and performers I've noted here.

Somewhere along the way, you took something in your head and put it out into the world. And somewhere along the way, I was able to hear you. You made some tough things more tolerable, you made confusing moments clearer, you made average days more special, and you made great times stick with me forever.

I cannot thank you enough for sharing your gifts.

There are also many people who contribute to a life becoming a story and a story becoming a book. I want to extend a warm and heartfelt thank-you to my editor, Elizabeth, who read my jumble of clumsy anecdotes and saw something worth reading. I knew I was lucky to work with you when I submitted the first of many "final" drafts and secretly felt there were three areas where I could have done better and a week later you reached out to say, "there are three areas where I think we can do better." Thanks for pushing me, Coach. To my collaborator, Steve Eubanks, I want to say that going back to our very first shared draft, I couldn't tell where my words stopped and yours started. If anyone asks me what good "collaboration" means in book writing, I can't think of a better definition than that. To Joe, Ann, Emily, and Jenny, who took the time to read this story and tell me where I needed to get better, I look up to you as storytellers. I'm grateful for your honesty, friendship, and laughter. Mostly the laughter.

My family has been mentioned throughout, but one more shoutout can't hurt. I read in a card one of you gave me "The miracle isn't that you finished, it's that you had the courage to start." Whatever "courage" I might have had to start this whole deal is because of your unconditional love and support.

To the Knights, PBs, Stephs, Toms, Tinas, Reubens, Cynthias, and all those unnamed who ever took a chance on me, the finished book in your hand would just be thoughts in my head without your trust. I love my soundtrack because it's filled with memories of you.